Northern portion of 1950s Flint, Michigan
map courtesy of the personal collection of the Morrow family

PROUDLY MADE
in FLINT, MICHIGAN

where my story begins

Michael Morrow

Morrow Books

Grafton, Illinois

The views expressed in this publication are those of the author and do not necessarily reflect the official policy and position of the City of Flint, Michigan, historically or currently; nor does it imply an endorsement of this publication by the City.

Copyright © 2020 by Michael R. Morrow

Published in the United States by
Morrow Books • Grafton, Illinois

Paperback ISBN 978-1-7356889-0-9
E-book ISBN 978-1-7356889-1-6

FIRST EDITION

www.morrowbooks.com

This book is dedicated to my grandchildren.

This is my story.

FOREWORD

Crisp winter morning in Flint, Michigan.

No one else on the steep, scary, snow-covered hills called the Hogbacks. My best friend and I wildly zipping down the ragged, jagged path until—Wham!

I'm unconscious. Knocked out cold by the hard ice at the bottom. Our tobogganing adventure ended before it had barely begun.

My friend managed to drag me to the top of the hill and drive me home. They fixed my face at the hospital, but I'm here largely because of my heroic first responder, Mike Morrow.

I've had the pleasure, and sometimes the pain, of Mike's camaraderie for more than six decades. From the very beginning, I could always count on him to be an avid adventurer, a fierce protector and, most importantly, a loyal friend.

Across my forty-year career in professional leadership development, I have seen many great leaders and Mike is no exception. Natural-born talent can only take you so far. Your decisions take you the rest of the way. Mike's choices and the lessons he learned while growing up make him a timeless and intriguing study in leadership development.

If you are a young, aspiring leader searching for a way forward, there are lessons for you in this book:

First, many heroic and exceptional individuals start out just like you. Young heroes-in-training can provide important guidance to their peers through genuine friendship. If you're not already one of them, surround yourself with people like that.

Second, even aspiring heroes make mistakes. If you learn from them, you will not just survive, you will thrive. Some lessons can only be learned through embarrassing or scary blunders. And, you can grow through these as Mike did.

Third, aspiring heroes are creative, big picture thinkers with great vision and heart. Your street smarts can help you get to the truth and see through the baloney while putting others' needs ahead of your own personal gain or glory.

If you are a parent who is unsure about where your rambunctious, wild child is headed—there are insights for you as well. Mentoring and building character in your own kids (or someone else's) requires an enormous investment of care and patience. Mike's story aptly illustrates the familiar goal of one generation sacrificing for and investing in the next with the bold hope that their offspring will achieve greater success than they did.

If you are a history buff, you will appreciate Mike's dynamic episodes set against the backdrop of a Midwestern boomtown in the 1950s and 60s. In that era, our nation's industrial pulse was strong in Michigan and its heart was in Flint for a few golden decades. The number of cars and trucks rolling off the lines mirrored the number of people streaming into "Vehicle City" for good jobs, benefits, and a promising future for their family.

Just as Flint's factories shaped the automotive industry, Flint's neighborhoods and families shaped the character of its youngest residents. Despite our hometown's economic boom, happy endings were not guaranteed. Mike and I grew up in a time and place where anything—good or bad—was possible. It all hinged on one's choices and the determination to see them through. Not so different from today.

Finally, Mike's candid account of a boy becoming a man resonates because each of us is a product of our family and upbringing, the social norms of our time, and our hometown. This heartfelt story is for everyone who was Proudly Made in Flint, Michigan— or in your hometown, U. S. A.

—Jim LaVictoire
September 1, 2020

CONTENTS

PROUDLY MADE in FLINT, MICHIGAN
where my story begins

CHAPTER ONE

We could have been killed at the Hogbacks.

If you've read the Foreword, you deserve to know the full story about that unforgettable episode in all its gory detail.

The winter after we graduated from high school, Jim and I were looking for an adventure. We piled into my car with a toboggan in the trunk and headed for the Hogbacks, a series of old gravel pits and hills dotted with scrub underbrush. In our expert opinion, we figured they'd be perfect for our next conquest.

I parked the car down near the road. We hauled the toboggan through fresh snow. Our deep tracks left a wandering imprint of our search for just the right hill. The wilderness, blanketed in thick silence, dared us to explore just beyond the next rise.

After trudging for about half a mile, we found it! Our perfect hill towered at least seventy-five feet overhead with a jaw-dropping, fifty-degree slope ending abruptly where its base met a frozen pond. It was the highest hill around and, therefore, the only one that would do.

We muscled our way to the top and surveyed our surroundings through the eyes of two old sledding pros.

After all, we had cut our teeth zooming down Iroquois Hill in town. We upped the ante when we barreled down the huge hill of the Flushing Golf Course—at night. Conquering this intimidating Hogback would complete our triple crown of sledding.

Jim lined up the toboggan with its nose poking over the steep drop off. He sat down at the front and tucked his feet under the curl, inside the sled's chains, effectively trapping himself.

Jim seemed calm and determined; I was a little nervous. The hill looked a lot higher from the top. Not wanting to sit down, I half crouched behind Jim, hanging onto his shoulders. At the first hint of danger, I was ready to jump off.

The frozen pond at the base of the hill suddenly seemed a very long way down. We took one last look at each other and bravely shoved off. Slicing through the icy air, our sled was a bullet.

WHOOOSHHH!

Something was wrong. We were going way too fast. I had just started to think about jumping off when we torpedoed, nose first, into the thick pond ice at breakneck speed.

The toboggan hit with a bone-jarring CRRRUNCH! I was catapulted high into the air—sailing over Jim—and landed about twenty feet beyond the sled. I lay there breathless, hurting, and confused.

What just happened here?

I sat up and looked back at the crash site. Jim was facedown on the ice, spread-eagled, feet still tangled in the chains. He wasn't moving.

I scrambled over to him, yelling, "Jim? JIM! Are you okay?!"

Eerie silence greeted my frantic calls.

I rolled him over and gasped. His face had slammed hard into the ice and was covered in blood. He was out cold but breathing. I tried unsuccessfully to rouse him and panic set in.

We were alone in the middle of nowhere. Not a single person knew where we were. I was afraid to leave him to get help; he would freeze in no time. Terrified for his life, I prayed.

After a few seconds, I knew what needed to be done. I'd have to transport Jim out of danger on the sled—even though he was taller and heavier than me. I carefully untangled his bulky boots from the chains. Struggling against the layers of his winter clothing, I strained to roll him over onto the sled.

After what seemed to be an eternity, I managed to pull him back to where we'd parked. He was slowly waking up as I loaded him into the car. I rushed him home and turned him over to his mother. I'm sure she hated to see us walking—limping—through her front door— again. She took him to the hospital where they repaired the damage to his face.

This misadventure added one more incident to a long list of similar episodes that have punctuated our life-long friendship.

Jim and I, along with most of the kids we knew, had just enough freedom to explore nearly every corner of Flint in free-range fashion—by today's standards. However, we also had more than enough accountability for our actions that, in turn, developed our common sense, integrity, and respect for authority.

It took the better part of eighteen years, but we went from making mischief to making something of ourselves. But I'm getting ahead of myself.

My father holding me in 1951.   I'm holding my son, Christopher, in 1978.

It all began for me on March 24,1951, when I arrived at 1:30 in the afternoon. It's interesting to note that twenty-seven years later to the minute, my son, Christopher, would be born in Fort Leonard Wood, Missouri on March 24, 1978, at 1:30 in the afternoon.

My father, Richard Paul Morrow, was born in 1928 in Flint. My mother, Nathalia Klein, was born in 1926 in a wooden farmhouse near the little town of New Lothrop, Michigan. They met at a dance after World War II (WWII) and the rest, as they say, is history.

They were married in 1950 and took a honeymoon drive up to the Michigan Upper Peninsula. Then they crossed the Straits of Mackinac on the ferryboat since the Mackinac Bridge had not yet been built. After their honeymoon, they bought our home at 813 West Baltimore Boulevard in Flint, moved in, and settled down to married life.

My father had a good job in the AC Spark Plug factory and my mom was a beautician. When I was born, Mom quit her job and took care of the household. The following year, on April 24, my brother Ken was born.

Dad came from a large family of twelve children and he was second from the youngest. Being one of the youngest, he was picked on by his older siblings, but they also looked out for him.

My father told me stories of growing up in the Great Depression of the 1930s when money was scarce and everyone worked hard to help keep food on the table.

I remember one story in particular. When he was about six years old, his father gave him a dime. He was so happy he bought some candy and a comic book. His older sisters berated him for taking their father's last dime, scolding about all the things their dad had to give up in order to give him that dime. This unwanted attention made him feel angry and hurt when all he wanted to do was to enjoy his candy and comic book.

The Great Depression ended and war clouds loomed ominously on the world's horizon, creeping slowly toward our country. Life went on as usual until Sunday morning, December 7, 1941, when the Japanese bombed Pearl Harbor. The very next day, recruiting stations were flooded with volunteers. Every able-bodied young man, it seemed, wanted to join up and fight.

All of the Morrow boys served in the Navy in WWII. My dad enlisted as soon as he finished high school in 1944. He was assigned to the destroyer USS Fletcher (DD-445) in the Pacific Theatre from 1944 until the end of the war. My father, along with his shipmates, experienced the grueling and gruesome effects of combat up close and personal. I believe this changed young eighteen-year-old boys, like

▼ Dad in California after the war, proudly wearing his Pacific Theatre campaign ribbons with battle stars.

▲ Dad with his parents after graduating from the Great Lakes Naval Training Center before he shipped out to the Pacific.

my dad, in ways not fully understood back then. Today, we recognize these effects as Post Traumatic Stress Disorder (PTSD).

Along with millions of other young men, Dad was mustered out of the service when the war ended in 1945. He said his farewells to the shipboard strangers who had become his brothers in combat, uncertain of ever seeing them again. Once stateside, he finally made his way back home to Flint by train.

Dad never spoke much about his war years. The only stories he ever told us were humorous ones about colorful characters and practical jokes. As little kids, we really didn't know what his job was in the war. We only knew that he served on a destroyer in the Pacific and that he kept his uniform with its one row of ribbons hanging in his closet for the rest of his life. It was a solemn, solitary reminder of his wartime experience.

When I became an adult, Dad told me how he accidentally left his duffle bag on the DC3 airplane that transported him stateside. He lost all of his war mementos from the Pacific Theater as well as any photographs or reminders of his comrades, living or dead. The sad irony was that he had lost some of the best memories of his service time and

Dad's family photo taken in 1947. Dad is on the top row, far right.

he struggled to forget the worst ones.

Like many veterans who lived through the horrors of war when so many did not, he spent the rest of his life looking back on those days in the Pacific and searching for answers. He remained close with some of his shipmates until eventually, each one passed away, answering the last ship's bell.

Years later, during my own military service in the Army, I learned that were it not for the ultimate sacrifice of one heroic young sailor, the Fletcher and her entire crew—including my father—would have been lost. I would never have been born and my branch of the Morrow family would not exist today.

Upon his return, my grandmother called on my dad to get a job and help support the family since my grandfather had passed away the year before. Dad's older brothers started their own lives after WWII, making my dad the only son left at home.

He found a good job at the AC Spark Plug factory in Flint and took on the new responsibility of providing for his mother and younger siblings. Not even two years out of high school and my dad was already a combat veteran and a de facto head of household!

Dad didn't tell us much about growing up in his family. I only met his mother once, and that was when I was about five years old. Dad and Mom bundled my brother Ken and me up in heavy coats because it was winter.

I remember climbing an old, dark, spooky stairway with Mom yelling at me all the way up, "You'd better be good!"

We came into a room that seemed awfully small. Dad's mom was sitting by a stove and dressed in a dark-colored long dress with a black eye patch covering her right eye. Her hair was as white as snow.

I don't remember much except that Mom smacked me on the way down for not behaving. I was scared out of my mind and I think I started to cry when I saw Dad's mother. Sadly, that's the one and only memory I have of my grandmother. I never met my grandfather.

—\\\\—

When Dad met Mom in 1949, he was still working at the AC Spark Plug factory in Flint. Dad wanted to get out of the factory. He didn't like being cooped up doing the same repetitive job on an assembly line, so when the Flint Fire Department was hiring new firemen, he jumped at the chance to change jobs.

The story goes that he was too short and did not weigh enough to meet the minimum requirements. In those days, they weighed you and took your height with your clothes on, so Dad hedged it a bit.

The morning of the exam, he wrapped a chain around his waist and stuffed pot holders in his shoes so he could meet the minimum weight and height requirements. He passed and became a fireman. He was a good driver and drove the hook and ladder truck at Station Number 3 in downtown Flint.

Dad always told us stories of the fires he fought. He told us of the biggest fire ever to hit downtown Flint in the middle of winter, when every truck in the city responded. One morning after he got home, he told us that he saved six baby puppies and the mother dog that were trapped in the basement of a burning building. He went in and carried them all out.

One day we heard a siren that sounded like it was on our street.

Everyone ran outside and to our surprise, we saw Dad driving the big hook and ladder truck right in front of our house! He rang the bell and waved as the big red truck turned the corner and roared up the street. We were all so excited and very proud of our dad.

Another time there was a fire in our neighborhood and Dad was off duty. We walked over to where the crew was fighting the fire at a neighbor's home. Dad pointed out to us that the firemen were putting on air tanks with masks before going into the house. He said these were brand-new and would allow the men to breathe while being inside the smoke-filled house. He talked with his buddies and Ken and I felt really important being with Dad.

Dad was a fireman for over thirty years and during that whole time, he held the job as driver for the hook and ladder truck. He took the sergeant's exam when I was just a little guy and I remember he came home and said he didn't make it. I don't think he ever tried to take the exam again. He was happy being one of the guys.

I visited his last living sister, Joanne, in 2018 and she told me a couple of stories about Dad that I had never heard. In the mid 1950s, Dad responded to a fire with his brother, my uncle, Delaus. The fire

Dad at a fire in late 1950s using a pole to push in a wall of a house. This picture appeared in *The Flint Journal,* our city newspaper.

Fire station Number 3 with Dad's fire truck on the left.

was at their sister's home. Joanne had two children, a boy around age six and a little girl about age two.

They were standing by a floor-mounted kerosene heater when it suddenly exploded. The boy was burned on his face, upper body, arms and hands and the little girl was engulfed. I learned from my aunt that my father and uncle carried those children out of that burning house.

The little girl passed away later that evening at the hospital and the boy, my cousin, survived but was scarred for the rest of his life. My father never spoke of this harrowing experience, and it wasn't until many years later that I learned of his heroic actions that fateful evening from his sister.

In later years, Dad also worked as the cook for his shift at the firehouse. He loved making chop suey, tacos, and pecan rolls, but his signature recipe was his chicken and dumplings. When I was home on leave from the Army one time, I was wise enough to ask him to teach me how to make them.

He said it was simple and he taught me how. To this day, I love making them with our grandchildren.

CHAPTER TWO

My mother, Nathalia Klein, was born in 1926

in a wooden farmhouse on a 200-acre dairy farm near New Lothrop, Michigan. She had everyone call her by her nickname, Pat.

Like Dad, she was also from a large family—and, coincidentally, the second youngest of twelve children! Her father's family had come from Germany and settled on a farm that was one mile down the road from his father's farm.

Mom would tell the story of how her 'Pubba' (her name for her father, my grandpa) would walk the one mile every night after supper to check on his mom and dad and their farm. She told stories of living in the old wooden farmhouse. It was so full of cracks that in the winter, the cold wind would howl and come right into the house. Mom

◀ Nathalia Klein, 1948.

▲ Mom came from a large farm family in Chesaning County, Michigan. Mom is second from the left, the last girl standing in the line.

Mom is third from the left.

said Grandpa could be heard yelling to the girls at night to close those windows! I learned that this big burly man also had a softer side. In the winter, he would sit in his rocker and crochet.

Mom loved to visit the farm and it seemed that we were there almost every Sunday. Grandpa's New Lothrop farm was about a thirty-minute drive from our home in Flint.

We would head out there after early church and spend the day. My mom really liked it there. All of her sisters and their husbands would also be there to visit. My dad always hung with the men, playing cards, drinking, and eating.

We kids would run wild outside the whole time. I felt sorry for the adults who just sat around and talked. Didn't they know that a wonderful world awaited them just outside the back door? Looking back, these were the best years—visiting Grandpa's farm.

Riding in the car on our way to the farm always filled me with anticipation. My attention and gaze were constantly directed to the world outside the car window and I would mentally check off familiar landmarks. My brother and I would sing out when we saw a well-known barn or that certain old truck hidden somewhere along the way.

We knew we were very close to the end of our journey when we could see the church spire at the country crossroads. We craned our necks out the window of our 1955 Chevy as we turned left at the church, looking up at the top of the spire with awe, knowing that the farm was just down the road.

Dad would always drive a little slower as we approached the farm. It sat off on the right hand side of the road and we could make out the barns and outbuildings over the rows of green corn.

The fieldstone house sat on a slight hill about one hundred feet from the road. Two large elm trees stood as silent sentinels at the head of the dirt driveway. The stone house had pink trim and rose-colored shingles, and stood proudly against the blue August sky as a testimonial to my grandfather's architectural and masonry skills.

The main entrance to the house was on the left as we drove up the long dirt driveway. On the right was a bright flower garden that followed the entire length of the driveway right up to the barn. This garden always had row upon row of multicolored blooms, and my favorites to this very day are the zinnias.

Over from the flowers and next to the corn running the entire length of the driveway, purple Concord grapes grew in huge, sweet clusters hanging on the fencerow set up to support them.

The garden was a bounty of different sights and tastes. To a young boy, there was no better place to start the farm adventure than by exploring the rows of colorful flowers. Sampling all the tasty fruits and vegetables fueled my many hours of outdoor amusement.

Between the house and the barnyard, stood a windmill. My brother and I would always stop at it on our way to the barn. It was covered in the bright orange flowers of trumpet vines that had a huge thick twisted trunk at the base and stretched to the top of the windmill.

The leaves swayed in the breeze and took on a living quality. One could almost imagine the tentacles of some living green monster that had sprung up out of the ground and were slowly engulfing the tower in their quest for freedom.

Looking up, it seemed as if the green vines and bright flowers were waving at me, inviting us to climb the old weathered steel tower and touch the white fluffy clouds floating overhead.

The air was always alive with the buzzing of hundreds of bees fly-

Grandpa William Klein's farm, taken by Dad, circa 1958.

ing from flower to flower to gather nectar.

Across from the windmill on the other side of the barn walkway was a stone-lined pond that my grandpa made from huge fieldstones. The stones were bigger than we were; but looking back, everything is bigger than you are when you're small.

Ken and I climbed the largest rock closest to the barn and played a game, walking around the top of the stones and trying very hard to keep our balance. We favored falling on the lawn instead of in the pond if we slipped.

We usually only completed one rotation before our excitement peaked. It was time to go to the barn! We jumped off the rocks (or

Grandpa's original wooden farmhouse with his family gathered among the peonies.

After WWII, Grandpa and his sons built their new home from the stones taken out of his fields.

picked ourselves up from where we fell) and ran down the path, leaving behind the windmill and pond.

There was an old fence that divided the barnyard from the home yard. This fence had large square stone corner pillars. The fence itself was overgrown with big round flowering bushes; the kind that could hide a camp or a secret Army base underneath. We usually stopped and checked our campsite to ensure that everything was in order.

Once our curiosity had been satisfied, we left the secret camp and headed out past the old fence to the real fun—the barnyard.

Grandpa raised dairy cows. We could smell the aroma of cow manure as soon as we got out of the car. Entering the barnyard took us to a world of awe and wonder.

Immediately on our left was a large red granary barn that also served as the lean-to garage for Grandpa's big old Buick. The sliding door on the barn was usually half open, inviting us to wander in, explore, and smell the dusty odors of grain and stale lubricating oil. We usually stopped and looked in the door on our way to our primary objective, the dairy barn.

Grandpa was of German descent, so everything was always orderly and well-maintained on his farm. His barn and outbuildings were painted farm red with bright white trim around the doors and windows. The large dairy barn was directly at the end of the driveway. We ran across the dirt parking lot to the barn.

The barn was massive! It had a great, single sliding door in the front facing the driveway with a small open door above it that allowed us to look into the hayloft. The barn sat with its longest length parallel to the highway and at a right angle to the house.

There were windows along the front and a small milk parlor on the far right side. On the left rear side of the barn sat the silo, a silent sentinel, sturdy and powerful, peeking over the top of the tin barn roof.

Grandpa and Grandma Klein. Grandma Klein passed on in 1959.

Grandpa standing next to the trumpet vine-covered windmill.

Left to right: Ken, Bob, and Mike sitting on the rock garden wall that Grandpa built.

Entering the barn, we were transported to another realm with its unique sights, sounds and smells. The cows were always grazing in the fields during the day, so we rarely ran into them in the barn.

Through the dim light filtering through overhead cracks in the hay loft and the cobweb covered windows, we could make out the milking stalls. Two rows of steel pipe stalls with strange-shaped metal holding collars awaited our inspection.

We were immediately overcome with the pungent odor of urine and manure, causing us to gag and our eyes to burn. We squinted our eyes until our senses gradually became accustomed to the smells and the dim light. Our ears picked up the sounds of flies buzzing and the occasional mooing of cows from the feedlot or pastures out back.

Ken and I quickly made our way to the stairs in the corner of the barn and climbed up to the hayloft. Dust sparkled and floated in the golden sunbeams throughout the length of this massive cavern.

Above our heads, the underside of the tin roof seemed to stretch up forever. We could hear the chirping and singing of barn swallows and sparrows from their nesting places throughout the barn.

The loft always had hay bales, sometimes reaching up to touch the roof. The smell of newly mowed hay and grass assailed our senses as we explored this secret fortress.

On the left end of the barn near the silo was an open door for load-

Grandpa's dairy barn.

Grandpa's cows grazing in his field. Background, left to right: the windmill, granary and big red dairy barn.

ing hay. Standing here, we surveyed the rest of our kingdom laid out below our feet. Our view took in the other large wooden barn that was actually a machine shed and work area, with interior walled corncribs. Outside, there was a metal scrap pile and of course, the tractors. My brother and I played for a while in the loft, then realized that time was of the essence and we needed to head to the machinery shed

Grandpa worked his farm with teams of horses in the old days and I have seen pictures of him with his team and stone sled loaded with rocks that he had cleared from the fields. The horses were only a memory when my brother and I started to visit the farm.

Grandpa had traded his horsepower for tractor power. Grandpa had two Farmall H tractors that he used to work the farm; they were big, red, and beautiful. I was drawn to them like steel to a magnet.

We spent many hours "driving" those tractors, pretending we were plowing fields, picking corn, and moving loads of hay. I never tired of climbing up onto them, swinging up into the seat, and gripping the big steering wheel.

Every time we visited the farm we found the tractors in a different spot, as if they were whispering, "Come and play on me over here. We can pretend we're driving out to beat the thunder clouds!"

Grandpa also had a little Ford 8N tractor. In later years, he got a

Grandpa's children playing in the yard of the old wooden farmhouse. Grandpa moved the farmhouse and built his new stone home on the old foundation and basement water cistern. The corner of the big barn is on the right. Uncle Allerd is on the bike and my mom is behind the baby on the blanket. Notice there is no Trumpet vine on the windmill. Circa late 1920s or early 30s.

Grandpa's family just before WWII. Grandpa is at lower right with my mom on his left looking over her sister's shoulder.

Mom and Dad, center, on their wedding day in early 1950.

Farmall 350 wide front tractor and an older 1952 Ford grain truck. There was always something new and exciting to see, do, and experience on the farm—fertile ground for an active boy's imagination.

The best part of our visits was that no one ever checked up on us and we played the entire day away, except for dinner.

We always dreaded hearing Dad yell for us to come on up to the house, because that meant it was time to go.

The ride home always seemed short; we knew that the following day brought school and routine, but for that one day a week we were free and happy.

—⟋⟍—

On one visit to the farm, Ken and I went into the big red wooden granary next to the garage. We looked into the grain bins and we saw a nest of baby mice.

We decided to take the mice home with us but knew if we asked Dad, he would say no.

So we hatched the idea of putting the mice in the car's ashtrays for the ride home, afterwards collecting them and putting them in a box.

Dad was driving a 1955 blue and white Chevrolet hardtop that he bought brand new. He was very proud of that car. The car was a four-door sedan and had a little ashtray nestled in each of the armrests of the front and back doors. We put a mouse in each ashtray and went back to playing.

When it was time to go home, we got in the car. Ken and I were in back and Mom was up front holding baby Bob. We waved goodbye and started the drive home.

After about two minutes, Ken and I sneaked a peak in our ashtrays to see the baby mouse nestled inside. The little ashtray door made a soft squeaking sound as it opened.

We were thrilled and not too bright. We kept opening and closing the ashtrays, giggling and whispering and squirming around with glee. This was easy to do since there were no seat belts back then.

Dad finally asked what the hell we were doing back there.

Of course, we said, "Nothing."

Left to right: Bob, Mike, and Ken exploring Grandpa's barn.

Mom said we were looking in the ashtrays and as if on cue, she opened her ashtray and looked inside.

She screamed and Dad almost ran off the road. She was sobbing that there was a mouse in the ashtray. Dad opened his ashtray. Behold, he found one, too!

Now Mom was in a full panic as she sobbed and yelled at Dad to pull over and get rid of the mice!

Dad pulled off the road and got out of the car. He started with his ashtray, yanking it out and dumping the mouse. Now we were crying in the backseat, Mom was shrieking in the front seat, and Dad was yelling as he yanked Mom's ashtray.

He went around to each of the car's ashtrays, dumping the mice. Once the mouse frenzy was finished, Dad got back in the car and we continued our ride home. Mom quietly sobbed in the front seat, holding baby Bob closely while suspiciously eyeing the ashtray.

So what went wrong with our plan? Why did we get caught? Why did those backseat ashtrays squeak in a new car?

They squeaked because they got wet and had rusted.

How did this happen, you ask?

Bob walking in Grandpa's yard.

The answer is simple.

Dad took Ken and me with him in the 1955 Chevy one Saturday to estimate a painting job. We were too young to go in with him, so he parked the car in the street and left us sitting in the back seat.

While he was gone, we really had to go to the bathroom but we were told we could not get out of the car.

So what did we do?

We pulled the backseat ashtrays out of the armrests, opened the little lids, and peed in them.

They filled up very fast and didn't hold a lot. We scooted to the open back window and dumped them outside. We probably did this about six times each until we were all finished, getting our fingers and those new ashtrays good and soaked.

When Dad came back, he asked how we were doing and we said fine. Those ashtrays rusted and squeaked from that day on.

—⁂—

We always seemed to get into trouble while having fun. Another time, we were with a couple of cousins playing hide and seek in

Left to right: Bob, Mike, and Ken eating lunch in Grandpa's sunroom.

Grandpa's farmhouse basement. It was an old concrete basement with lots of old, dusty junk. It was my turn to hide and I was looking for a good hiding place.

I climbed up on an old table and looked into a large hole in the concrete wall. I was surprised to see a big room filled with water. I didn't know it then, but this was the farm's cistern that held hundreds of gallons of water that was pumped in by the windmill.

It was dark and deep, and if I fell in, I probably would not have gotten out. Fortunately I decided that it wasn't a good place to hide and climbed down.

I finally found an old wooden cupboard standing on the floor. I squeezed in and slammed the door shut.

It was very dark inside and I started to get scared. I couldn't move and I thought I was having trouble breathing. I pushed the door to get out, but it wouldn't budge. I tried again harder, frantically, but still it didn't budge.

I was in total darkness, I couldn't move and I panicked!

I started screaming and hitting the door as hard as I could in those cramped quarters.

After what seemed like an eternity, the door suddenly opened, filling my space with light.

Relieved, I heard Ken say, "So there you are!"

I fell out and collapsed on the floor, breathing heavily and feeling like I had just crawled out of a mineshaft. The cupboard door had an old-time latch that you had to turn in order to make it open. I didn't know that. I was grateful to Ken for getting me out.

—⁓—

It wasn't too long after that episode that Ken needed my help. We were playing outside by the granary one day and decided to look into Grandpa's garage.

We wiped the dust from the old windows on the wooden door and peeked in at his big, beautiful Buick Roadmaster. Ken liked big boats, Buicks, and Cadillacs. I preferred trucks. Of course, we both loved Dad's 1955 Chevy.

We turned and started down a small sidewalk that ran the length of the garage and was partially hidden by bushes. The sidewalk was very narrow, making it difficult to walk and not get slapped in the face by branches. We swatted at the branches and suddenly found ourselves at the end of the path.

Standing in front of us and blocking our way was a little skinny house. The house was made of wood and in dire need of paint. There was one narrow door that was leaning open, beckoning us to come a little closer and look in.

We crept nearer and peeked into the gloomy interior. We saw a wooden bench that was built into the back wall, but this bench had two big holes in it. We wondered what kind of playhouse this was. I probably told Ken to sit on the bench.

The next thing I knew, he was yelling, "Help me, Mike!"

Sure enough, he had slipped through one of the holes and was holding on for dear life. His butt and backside had slipped into the hole and he was holding himself up by his elbows and feet. He looked as scared as I felt.

I screamed, "I'll go get Dad," and took off running down the path.

I ran very fast, turning at the windmill and dashing up to the house. I don't remember what I said, but Dad dropped everything and came racing with me. He quickly passed me and I had trouble keeping up.

We sped down the path as fast as we could, swatting branches aside.

We stopped in front of the little house, catching our breath, and Dad said, "Well, where is he?"

I looked into the house and it was empty. Ken was gone. Did he get himself out?

I started to say something when we heard a noise coming from inside the hole where Ken had been just a few minutes ago. Dad looked into the hole, and sure enough, there was Ken at the bottom of a pit. He looked despondent as the sunshine lit up his little face.

The good news was that the old outhouse was no longer in use and the poop pit was dry. It was perched on a small hill and there was a clean-out opening in the back of the pit where Ken could crawl out. After he came out, we both got yelled at. Another fun day on the farm.

—⟋⟍—

My visits to Grandpa's farm were few and far between once I graduated from high school and started working. They had stopped, except for one visit when I had joined the Army in July 1971.

Grandpa sold his farm to his next-door neighbor in late 1972 and divided the proceeds among his children. Grandpa went to live with my Aunt Lale and Uncle Bob in their home near Flushing and passed on shortly after that.

I remember visiting him one other time at Uncle Bob's house when I was home on leave before being assigned overseas. He was sitting on the couch and my mom and a couple of her sisters were in the kitchen whispering.

Seems they were all upset because Grandpa had snuck off that morning. He'd gone to Dalton Airport, a little local dirt strip runway with a few hangers, and had taken a ride in a small Cessna airplane.

I remember those women dramatically wringing their hands and asking him in tearful voices why he would do such a thing. He could

My grandpa, William Gustave Klein, lived from 1884 to 1974.

have been killed!

My grandpa, who was around ninety-five at the time, chuckled and said, "Because I've never been up in a plane and I always wanted to do it."

This seemed to send them into more worried chatter and clucking as they went back to the kitchen.

I looked at Grandpa and he smiled at me, as if to say, "I've still got it!"

I miss my grandfather's farm and all that it meant to me. Those fond memories drive a desire in me to find a farm of my own. I would like to climb a hayloft once again, wander in a garden and play with tractors.

I'd like to have a place for my grandchildren to visit where they can have adventures and build memories.

My grandpa has been gone since 1974 but I think of him every time I see a red barn, a Farmall tractor, or smell a zinnia.

CHAPTER THREE

Our home was located in the northwest section of Flint near the major intersection of DuPont and Pierson Streets at 813 West Baltimore Boulevard. The area was divided into blocks that were not very large. The homes were a mix of older homes and those that were quickly built after WWII to accommodate the large number of returning veterans. They and others were all looking to land good jobs in the thriving Flint auto industry.

Our house was a two-story wood frame and siding construction with a dirt driveway and no garage. It had wooden screens and storm windows, a coal furnace, and no air conditioning.

Our home at 813 W. Baltimore Boulevard, in Flint.

Richard and Nathalia Morrow on our front porch. Dad did all of the maintenance on the house and Mom did all of the cleaning and cooking.

Dad did all of the repair and upgrade work on our home himself. Over the years, he replaced the coal furnace, built a garage, and extended the kitchen. He also built bedrooms in the basement, painted the home and garage every few years, and poured a concrete driveway.

He was a good provider and a hard worker. He helped neighbors with their home improvement projects for reduced pay or sometimes for free. He took great pride in our home's appearance and it showed.

I grew up a block away from the Flint Amusement Arcade Park and two blocks away from Devil's Lake. The amusement park had rides, games, a skating rink, and a wooden roller coaster. It was a going concern until it closed in the early 1960s.

Dad took Ken and me for some rides and a walk through the park one evening. The sights, sounds, and smells were intoxicating, and all this was only one block from our home!

My brother Ken was only a year younger than I, and we were playmates. The next oldest brother was Bob, but being even younger, we didn't play with him very much.

The next kids in our family were John, Don, and Mary. This group came along when I was in late middle school and high school, so I

My sister Mary riding her tricycle.

didn't really interact much with them either.

Dad would occasionally surprise us with little gifts and toys. One time I remember a couple of weeks before Christmas, he came home from work with two toys—one for Ken and one for me.

He was wearing his fireman's uniform and he looked down at me as I was playing in the living room and said, "Here you go."

He handed me a hard yellow plastic International dump truck. I loved that truck! He grinned, seeing our faces light up as we played.

One day, Dad came home with two fairly long boxes for Ken and me. When we opened our boxes, we were astonished to see a Mattel Shootin' Shell Rolling Block Indian Scout Rifle! We gasped and squealed with delight.

The rifle came with a bandolier of leather with realistic bullets held in cartridge loops. The little plastic bullets would actually shoot out of the gun!

To make the shooting noise, we placed a round Greenie Stick-em cap to the back of the bullet. Next, we cocked the hammer, and then rolled back the block on the rifle, just like the real thing. This opened the breach and we inserted a bullet into the breach and rolled the block back in place with a thumb. When we pulled the trigger, the hammer fell, striking the cap and making a loud Bang!

The bullet was pushed out of the barrel at the target by a small hidden spring in the shell casing. We then re-cocked the hammer, rolled back the block, and the empty shell casing would fly out, just like a real gun. Load another "live" bullet and shoot all over again. What a blast!

Armed with this authentic replica of the real rifle, Ken and I went to work playing "Cowboys and Indians." We transformed the living room into a fort from the Wild West by moving Dad's footstool to the far end of the room. This provided all the cover we needed as we laid out our bandoliers of bullets.

Just then we saw Indians climbing down the staircase trying to sneak into the fort! We started shooting and reloading. Bullets and empty shell casings went flying!

Suddenly Ken yelled, "I'm running low on ammo!"

I did a quick check and saw that I was, too.

We took aim at a couple more Indians, and as they regrouped, we reloaded our rounds. We played at this game all afternoon, never tiring of shooting, loading, and reloading those beautiful rifles.

—⋙—

After the amusement park finally closed and was boarded up, we snuck down there in the summer and explored the old empty buildings and assorted junk that was left behind. Over the years, the vacant park became choked with weeds and bushes and turned into a really neat old ghost town that was always fun to play in.

One of the things we liked to do in the park area was to build tree houses. There was plenty of material around from the old amusement park and we borrowed a hammer, saw, and some nails from Dad's workbench.

We cut trails and secret paths through the undergrowth off the old service roads. In this secluded area, we built several tree houses over the years, with the best one being at the entrance to the old skating rink. That tree was very tall and old, with many good branches sticking out to accept platforms and handholds to help us up while climbing.

One day, I was working on the main platform, a small flat wooden section in the crook of the tree that was as high as the top of the neighboring telephone poles. I was adding another board and nailing.

Nick and his buddy, Rick, decided that they needed to cut off a limb that was in the way of future expansion of the platform. The limb was level with the platform we were working on. They picked up the saw and started to cut.

The swishing sound of the saw went on for several minutes. I realized that the sawing had stopped and it felt like the platform was shaking. I looked back over my shoulder to see what was going on. I saw Nick and Rick jumping up and down on the limb that they were cutting and holding onto another branch above their heads. They were laughing and grunting as they jumped on the cut limb, trying to get it to break off and fall down. I turned around and went back to hammering.

I worked for about fifteen seconds then turned back to see how they were doing. I saw nothing. What I mean is, I saw empty blue sky where just a few seconds ago, those two were jumping up and down

Left to right: Mike, Bob, and Ken camping in the back yard.

on the branch. It took me a second to realize that they were gone. I quickly crawled over to the edge of the platform and looked down.

There they were, splayed out on the ground so far below with the broken tree limb entangled around them. They didn't move. I was terrified that they were dead. The silence was deafening.

Suddenly Nick started to groan and move, then Rick did also. I clambered down the tree and was amazed to find that they were both okay. We decided to call it quits on the tree house for that day.

—⟋⟍—

One day, Ken was with a friend at a tree house they built on the other end of the park. They were working on it when Denny Branson and his gang came by. They were the local teen gang, complete with combed-back hair, cigarettes, and leather jackets. They grabbed Ken's friend and started roughing him up. They called for Ken to come down, but he refused. Denny sent one of his guys up the tree and he grabbed Ken and held him out over the edge, ready to drop him at his leader's command.

For some reason, they asked his name and he said he was Ken Morrow.

Denny looked at him and asked, "Are you Mike Morrow's brother?"

Ken said he was, and Denny told his henchman to let him go because he was my brother. Ken was ever so grateful and he and his buddy skedaddled.

Why did the gang leader let my brother go?

Earlier that summer, Denny Branson and his gang had trolled our street corner where we were playing kickball. I saw Denny hide a large bayonet knife under his jacket near the fence where he and his guys dropped their belongings. When they were ready, they came out and took over the game.

Just then a police car stopped and the officers started questioning the gang. While everyone was watching the action with the police, I moved over by the fence. I took Denny's knife and hid it in some tall grass about ten feet away.

The police looked through the gang's clothing by the fence. They

Hamming it up for a photo in back of our house. Left to right: Bob, Ken, neighbor Tommy, and Mike.

found nothing but cigarettes and they eventually moved on. Denny had a very strange look on his face. I could see by his expression that he was puzzled about that knife. I went over and told him what I had done and showed him where his knife was. From that day on, I was okay in Denny's eyes.

—⟶⟵—

On the nights when Dad was sleeping at the fire station, Mom would always call him just before bedtime to give him a report. If he had time, we'd get to say hi on the phone. Our phone was an old, pale green rotary dial phone and I still remember our old Flint phone number: Sunset (SU) 7-8118.

On several occasions, the fire alarm would go off in the background and Dad would have to hang up abruptly and jump on his fire truck to respond to the alarm.

One night, I was playing my trombone over the phone for him. When I finished, I picked up the phone and asked, "Did you like it?" All I heard was the dial tone.

"I'm sure he had a fire to go to, " said Mom with a knowing smile.

—⟶⟵—

Ken and I joined the Boy Scouts and walked about a mile and a half to the meeting place by our school. One night we were walking home from the meeting and it was dark.

As we approached the intersection of Pierson and DuPont Streets, we saw a strange object hovering in the sky over the corner gas station.

It flew high above us and was shaped like a saucer with a dome in the middle. There was a single row of lighted windows around the lower portion of the dome. It was traveling toward Devil's Lake and would pass right over our house.

As we watched this strange object, Ken suggested that it was a flying saucer and I agreed. We picked up our pace, and with a quick glance left and right, we dashed across Pierson Street, our eyes still glued on the object.

Ken yelled that it was rotating; we bolted for home as fast as we could run. We lost track of it as it went over the lake.

Mom was sitting on the couch in the living room holding one of the babies and watching the black and white TV.

We erupted through the front door and breathlessly tried to describe, at the same time, the terrifying thing we had just witnessed. Finally, we blurted out that we had tracked a flying saucer all the way home and that it was over Devil's Lake—right now!

Of course, the younger kids were startled by the commotion and began to cry. We must have been quite a sight—wide-eyed, all out of breath, and shouting out this crazy story. Mom panicked and started crying and screaming (she did that a lot). She yelled at us to move the dining room table in front of the door to block the aliens that surely must be coming from the direction of the lake.

We piled the furniture against the front door, all the little kids cried, and Mom dialed the phone to call Dad at the fire station. She was hysterical.

By the time Dad came to the phone, she was sobbing, the babies were howling, and she was screaming about aliens from Devil's Lake trying to break into our home.

Standing by the fortress we were building at the front door, I could hear Dad yelling over the phone. After several minutes, he finally managed to quiet Mom down and she hung up the phone.

She glared at Ken and me and told us to put the furniture back, grumbling, "You just wait until your father gets home!"

Somehow I figured we would be safe from Dad's wrath on this one, and I was right.

—m—

Mom was a wonderful mom, but she had difficulty coping with us little hellions. On leave from the service one time, I visited Aunt Francis (Dad's oldest sister). She told me that my mom had suffered a breakdown not long after Ken was born and that I'd come to live with her for a while.

I don't know where Ken went—he was a tiny baby, and I would have been just thirteen months old. To this day, I can still picture the inside of Aunt Francis' home—the kitchen, dining room and living room. She had a son, Richard, who was several years older than I was and everyone called him "Dickie."

I remember that Dickie got to open one present a night starting about five days before Christmas. These were presents that relatives had dropped off. By opening one a night before Christmas, it allowed him to appreciate that one gift, and Aunt Francis made him write a thank you note to the giver.

Left to right: Mike, Ken, and Bob on Easter morning.

Christmas morning at the Morrow home. Left to right: Bob, Mike, and Ken. Bob got the three big orange trucks and shovel, Mike has an Army set, and Ken is opening a fire truck set.

Our parents always made sure our holidays were special. Left to right: Bob, Ken, and Mike one fine Christmas morning.

One night, he opened a big present. It was an orange Hubley log truck with long brown logs kept in place on the trailer with a tiny chain.

I so loved the idea of spreading out Christmas that when we had our son, Christopher, he was introduced to the tradition we lovingly called "A Dickie Smith Christmas."

—␣␣␣—

Mom was always busy with a baby or preparing a meal, either lunch or dinner, when we got into trouble.

She yelled at me, rarely spanked me, but most often, she threatened me with, "Wait until your father gets home!"

And she always followed through on that threat. My dad was no sooner in the back door from the fire station or painting a house than Mom unloaded on him all the terrible things I'd done.

Ken was never mentioned in these frequent data dumps. He knew how to blend into the woodwork. The mood Dad was in and how much Mom dumped determined my punishment. Most often, he yelled, hit me, and that was it.

We lived very close to Devil's Lake. Mom and Dad made it clear that we were to stay away from that "bottomless" lake. Summer rumors were always flying around about who drowned in the lake and how it happened. Of course, no one could ever corroborate them and they just kept resurfacing.

One afternoon, Ken and I were playing outside in the front yard when suddenly there was a lot of commotion with loud emergency sirens. People started coming out of their houses and looking toward the lake. Some were even running down the street toward the noise.

We stood around in little clusters talking and watching the emergency workers by the lake. Suddenly, someone ran by and told us that little Gino, the boy who lived on the next block, drowned in the lake and they were searching for him.

The story took shape as others came by saying that Gino and his big brother, Nick, were on a homemade raft on the lake when the little boy fell in and went under the water. This was all very dreadful to us.

We kids felt like we were a part of this terrible, important happening as we watched and listened to the firsthand reports.

Suddenly, Ken and I spotted Dad driving home in his battered 1960 Chevrolet station wagon. He was covered in paint, having just finished working for the day, and was headed home to clean up and relax. We had to tell him!

We burst into action, running lickety-split across the street, waving our hands over our heads.

We shouted, "Dad! Dad!" as loudly as we could.

He saw us as he came to a stop at the corner of Winthrop and Baltimore, kitty corner from our home. He looked at us with a puzzled look on his face, which then turned into the start of a grin. He must have thought we were glad to see him.

We ran up to his open driver's window and yelled, "Dad! Guess who drowned in Devil's Lake?"

His grin turned to horror, and his face went pale, as he must have noticed that only two of his five children were standing in front of him.

Before he could say anything, we quickly blurted out, "Little Gino!"

He didn't move for a few seconds. In retrospect, he was probably trying to calm his heart rate.

We stood by the car, panting and looking like the true professional talebearers that we were, thinking how proud he must be of us for giving him this important news so quickly. He finally turned to us and told us in a very angry voice to get home.

—⟋⟍⟍—

Bad news traveled very fast in our little neighborhood. You knew whom you could count on and whom you should stay away from. Mr. Nickelson was one of the ones you could count on.

He lived on the next street with his family, just behind where our friends, Pat, and his little brother Mikey, lived with their mom, who was divorced. Pat was our age and little Mikey was just about two years old.

One fall evening, tragedy stuck. Pat and Mikey were home with their mom and it was cold in their house. She decided to start a fire in the fireplace and made several attempts, burning newspapers and twigs, to no avail.

She went out back and came in with a can full of gas. Pat and Mikey were standing next to her in front of the fireplace when she sloshed some gas in the fireplace.

There must have been embers burning because the gas immediately caught fire and exploded outward. The fire covered her legs, and Pat from the chest down. Little Mikey was engulfed in flames.

She screamed and I saw Mr. Nickelson running from his house into their burning home. Smoke was boiling out of the house as Mr. Nickelson came running out the front door holding little Mikey wrapped in his T-shirt, pushing Pat and his mother to safety.

The fire trucks arrived and they fought the fire. Pat and his mother survived with major burns. Little Mikey died that evening in the hospital.

I will never forget the image of Mr. Nickelson running into that burning house and carrying that little baby out the front door in his big angel arms. Like most of the men in our neighborhood, Mr. Nicholson was a WWII combat veteran.

—⁓—

We knew our neighbors and interacted with them. We had mostly good neighbors. Mr. Whitaker lived next door to us on the left. We mowed his lawn in the summer and shoveled his driveway and sidewalks in winter. He would always overpay us! We would ask for fifty cents and he would give us a dollar.

Mrs. McGilvery lived next door on the right. Mom told us she was a widow so we had to shovel her driveway and sidewalk for free.

Her "brother" came by often in his pickup truck to mow her lawn and do odd chores for her. Ken and I found out later in life that he was actually her boyfriend. Mom didn't want us to know she was divorced.

She was a very nice woman and always had a kind word for us. To this day, I still call the pretty purple-flowered bushes she had in front of her house "Mrs. McGilvery bushes."

Mr. McGonagall lived behind us. He had a big double lot and a TV antenna that reached into the sky about twenty feet above his house. Dad climbed that antenna and painted it for him on a regular basis.

Ken and I cut his lawn. He let us use his Lawn Boy power mower and he still paid us two dollars!

I recall Dad talking with him over the back fence, both of them smoking Camel cigarettes, when Mr. McGonagall turned to me and said, "Don't ever start smoking. You can feel the nicotine traveling in your bloodstream," as he traced his yellowed finger up his arm.

That spooked me, and I never forgot it.

—◠◠◠—

Dad was the disciplinarian in our home. His justice was usually swift, always included yelling, and some form of corporal punishment.

Mom was the screamer and threatened us with telling Dad, but she could also dish it out on her own without Dad's help. She had little pet names for us when she was really mad. My pet name was "Mock" and Ken's was "Dumber than Dirt."

One time, I did something that really got her going. She must have been having a seriously bad day, because she yelled, "That's it! You're going away to Reform School!"

Now all of us kids had heard about Reform School from Mom many times. The school had bars and cages. You wore prison-like uniforms and stayed locked up. Mom took great delight in telling us how these schools worked, and how they took bad boys away.

Well, she sat down by the phone in the living room and picked up the receiver. She opened the phone book and looked up a number.

By this time, I was getting a little nervous, as this had never happened before.

She dialed a number. I was too young to realize it then, but she was faking the call.

She spoke into the phone, "Yes, hello, is this the Reform School?"

When I heard that, I started crying and pleading, "I promise I'll be good. Please don't send me away!"

She told the imaginary person on the other end of the line that she

From the edge of our driveway, left to right: Don, John, Bob, Ken, and Mike. Baltimore Blvd. runs off the top left edge of the photo and ends at Devil's Lake. The Baldwin and Baltimore intersection behind us is where we played kickball.

had a really bad boy who needed to go to their school. Then she proceeded to improvise an entire conversation about what I had done.

Through my tears, I begged for her mercy sincerely enough that she finally said, "Just a minute, please."

She cupped her hand over the mouthpiece and asked me, "Are you going to be good?"

I promised her the moon—anything. "Just please don't send me there."

"We'll see," she said. Then she pretended to tell the person on the phone that she would give me one more chance. She hung up, but not before asking the person at the Reform School to please hold my cell—just in case.

She gave me a stern lecture and then sent me to my room.

Her truly Oscar-worthy performance for the Reform School ruse is still etched in my memory all these years later. She had certainly gotten my attention in that moment; however, not quite enough to effect any long-term change in my behavior.

With great relief, I quickly climbed up the stairs to go to my room when I noticed Ken wide-eyed and crouching at the top of the stairs where he had a ringside seat for the whole exhibition.

With a concerned look he said, "She almost got you that time."

I agreed, went to the room that I shared with Ken and Bob and stretched out on my bed to contemplate life.

—⟋⟍—

Sometimes I played with Ken and his friend, Larry Morgan. Larry lived on the next street over and we could see his house. We played a lot of games involving guns and any combination of cops and robbers, cowboys and Indians, and monsters. We didn't know what zombies were back then or we would have shot them, too.

One day we were playing in Larry's old wooden garage when he suddenly just stood still.

Ken said, "Come on, Larry!"

But he just stood rock still with a big grin frozen on his face. Suddenly he shook his pant leg and something brown dropped out of the bottom of his left pant leg with a soft little plop!

He grinned and said, "Okay, let's go," and took off running out of the garage, chasing an imaginary bad guy.

Larry didn't like to go into his house. Whenever he appeared, his mother would make him stay inside for the rest of the day.

—⟋⟍—

There were lots of kids in our neighborhood. Ken and I each had our own friends but sometimes we all played as a group. In the summer, we would go outside in the morning after our bowl of cereal and play until lunchtime.

After devouring our favorites, Campbell's tomato soup and Velveeta grilled cheese sandwiches; we headed back outside until Mom yelled for us to come home. With no cell phones or computers and very limited black and white TV, we were outside all day when the weather was good.

We explored the old abandoned amusement park, built tree houses and forts, and caught tadpoles in the swamp. When we were older, we rode our bikes everywhere and enjoyed the freedom and range to explore beyond the boundaries of our small neighborhood.

Garbage pickup for our neighborhood was on Monday. In the summer, Ken and I rode our bikes up and down the streets near our home to check out what the neighbors were throwing away. We learned from an early age that one man's trash is another man's treasure.

We took our two galvanized metal cans to the curb before breakfast. The lids became our shields when playing swords. One can was filled with kitchen scraps that were wrapped in newspaper since there were no plastic garbage bags back then. This can was usually the heaviest and smelled pretty bad. We had to rinse out this one after the pick up because there were usually lots of maggots in it.

The other can held metal, glass, wood and junk. There was no recycling collection in the 1950s, so everything from both cans went to the dump.

Once the cans were at the curb, we went back inside, ate breakfast, and got on our bikes. We had a route we followed, but if we spotted something really good, we made a beeline for it. The cans that held the junk often didn't have a lid.

We peered into each can with an experienced eye as we slowly rode past them, mentally evaluating the treasures within. When we found a not-too-broken toy or something we just had to have, we lifted it from the can. We had to be quick in order to beat the garbage trucks before they collected our treasures. Once we finished our route, we would take our trophies home.

The City used two kinds of orange 1958 Chevrolet Viking trucks. The first truck had an enclosed body on the back that was rounded on top. Across the back of the truck there was a large trough. Two garbage men picked up the cans containing the kitchen waste. These men rode on the back of the big truck like firemen. They jumped off, hefted the cans, and dumped them into the trough.

When this big trough was filled with disgusting, soupy slop, the man on the right side emptied it by pulling a lever. The trough slowly climbed up the rounded body, dripping slimy slop as it rose, and poured everything into an open slot at the top.

The empty trough would come back down and the process would start all over. There were always a lot of big flies buzzing around this truck like little alien spaceships around the mother ship.

The second truck was a dump truck with low sides. The men on this truck lifted and dumped the cans with the junk into the back.

As a side note, there was one enterprising individual we remember who tied big cans to the front and sides of his trash hauling truck. He would separate the bottles into one can, copper and other metals into another, and toys and useful items in the rest. He was a man ahead of his time—quite possibly one of the world's original recyclers.

We loved watching the men work as we stayed a couple of houses ahead of them. Neither of us wanted to be a garbage man, but we both wanted to drive those big, powerful, orange trucks.

—◊◊◊—

In our backyard, we had a very large cherry tree. It was the only tree in our yard and it was taller than our house. Dad, and the teen boy from across the street, built our garage from scratch, and the roof of the garage ended up right under the west side of the cherry tree. We loved climbing up the tree to get on the garage roof so we could pick the big, red, sweet cherries in late June and early July.

One summer afternoon, Tommy Montpas and I were picking cherries. I was on the roof and Tommy was higher up in the tree.

Suddenly, Tommy yelled down, "Hey, Mike, your mom is burning your kitchen again."

I looked toward the back of the house and saw Mom at the stove, wildly swinging a towel at the stovetop, trying to put out a small fire. Our dinner was most likely going up in flames. Chuckling, we shrugged and went back to picking cherries.

—◊◊◊—

Ken and I grew string beans in the little alley between our home and Mrs. McGilvery's fence. We used Dad's shovel to turn the ground and broke up the dirt clumps with the garden rake.

We planted six rows that ran parallel to the house. We watered them regularly with the garden hose and pulled the weeds that seemed to sprout up everywhere. It was hard work but we enjoyed watching the bushy green plants grow.

One day, we spotted beans growing. Lots of beans! We picked them, filling our buckets. Mom was really proud of us, and we all feasted on fresh green beans with melted butter for dinner that night.

—⁓—

Although we may have made jokes to the contrary, Mom was a good cook. She learned from her mom on the farm. We didn't have microwaves, frozen food, or prepared dinners; and we didn't eat fast food very often. Everything she made was from scratch and was either cooked on the stove or baked in the oven.

Our favorite meals were roast beef with carrots, potatoes, and onions slowly simmered in a big covered black pot in the oven; spaghetti and sauce with Kraft Parmesan cheese; macaroni and cheese; sweet corn on the cob in season; pancakes; and pork and beans with SPAM—a canned WWII-era 'delicacy' that consisted of precooked, ground-up pork shoulder and ham with some seasonings.

The bean meals were easy to make and we loved them. Mom put the pork and beans in a large pot, added molasses and brown sugar, and diced up a whole can of SPAM. She let the mixture simmer, and then served us full plates of beans for lunch or dinner.

When money was tight, she made pancakes for dinner. One night, she put pancakes on our plates. We were lathering them with butter when she suddenly realized that we were out of syrup.

We started to whine and she quickly grabbed the sugar bowl and started sprinkling sugar on our hot pancakes. The sugar blended with the melted butter.

Mom told us to stop whining and eat our dinner. She said, "This is how we ate them on the farm."

We tentatively took a first bite. It was wonderful! We ate all our pancakes and begged for more. To this day, Ken says he still prefers his pancakes with sugar.

Lunch consisted of a peanut butter and grape jelly or a Velveeta grilled cheese sandwich with soup, or a pork and bean sandwich with Miracle Whip.

We never went out to eat in a restaurant. We only went to places where we could eat in the car, like McDonald's, A&W Root Beer, or Coney Island stands. We were too fidgety and Mom felt she couldn't yell at us in a restaurant. The car offered the perfect solution. She could control us and no one could see how badly behaved we were.

—∿∿—

We always had popcorn when we went to the drive-in movies. Mom made the best popcorn in the world. To this day, I still make it exactly as she did.

She started by putting a little Crisco in a big pot on the stove. In a separate pan, she melted a stick of butter. Once the Crisco was melted, she added the yellow hulled popcorn and covered the pot. She had a large brown paper shopping bag open and waiting on the counter as the kernels exploded against the lid.

When the lid was bursting off the pot, she quickly dumped the fluffy kernels into the bag. She added the butter and salt, closed the bag, and shook it really well. It was ready when we saw butter stains appear on the outside of the bag, and the kitchen smelled of delicious, hot buttered popcorn.

If we were eating the popcorn at home, she divided it up into small bowls, perfect for sitting in front of our black and white TV. If we were going to the drive-in movie, she left the popcorn in the bag and took the bowls along.

To see a movie, we always went to a theatre or the drive-in. Movies weren't regularly broadcast on TV until later in the 1960s. We didn't have VCR's, DVD's, or Netflix. We went to drive-ins quite often growing up.

Dad took Ken and me to a movie theatre twice that I recall. Once we saw *The Guns of Navarone* and the other time we saw *The Longest Day*. All of our family movie outings were at the drive-in.

I remember one time when we were getting ready to go to the drive-in. Mom made the popcorn and filled the green thermos jug with

Kool-Aid while we kids got into our pajamas. We loaded up the car and headed out.

We arrived just as the sun was going down. Dad hooked up the car speaker to his door while we got out and went to play on the playground sets under the big screen. There were lots of other kids playing on the swings and slides, most of them in their pajamas.

Once the previews for coming attractions began, we all ran back to our cars. We wiggled and settled in, got our popcorn and watched the previews, followed by a double feature.

Over the years, we saw *Ben-Hur*, *The Ten Commandments*, lots and lots of westerns, Army movies, and science fiction movies. The two that scared me the most were *Them*, a really scary movie about giant ants, and *The Creature from the Black Lagoon*.

When we came home from watching the *Creature* movie, Dad took us upstairs to bed in the front bedroom. He tucked us in, said good night and headed back downstairs.

I told him I was scared.

He said it was only a movie and to go to sleep.

I was terrified. I lay there thinking that the creature was going to climb up the stairs and grab me, just like in the movie. I was getting ready to call for Dad when I heard a very familiar sound.

Drifting up the stairs was the very loud sound of my dad snoring. I reasoned that if the creature broke into our home, he would hear Dad snoring and go toward the sound of the noise. In the terrible fight that would surely ensue, Ken, Bob, and I would be able to run out of the house and get help while Dad was dealing with the creature. It made sense and I was able to get to sleep.

—ᴡ—

Dad loved the drive-in. He could smoke in the car, drink his beer, and see a couple of newly-released movies. There were a couple of ground rules for us kids: we only went to the concession stand if we had to use the bathroom, and only during intermission.

If we parked close enough to the concession stand, we could go to the bathroom on our own. Opening a car door during the movie was impolite to those around you because the dome light would come on and ruin their view.

One time at the drive-in, Bob had to go to the bathroom. He was in the back of the station wagon with Ken and me. Mom told him to hold it and he said he couldn't.

He started to do a little jig on his knees, holding the front of his pajamas. His timing was off; it was right in the middle of the first movie. He couldn't go to the concession stand by himself because we were parked farther away than usual.

We were surrounded by cars and no lights could be seen anywhere except the red dot glows from cigarettes. The movie was a really good western that Dad wanted to see.

He told Bob to hold it. When Bob started to wiggle and whine Mom came up with a brilliant idea—let him go in a milk carton! Dad told her to take care of it as his attention was focused on the big screen.

Mom just happened to have an empty one-quart cardboard milk carton. She opened the top, handed it to Bob, and told him to pee in the carton.

Bob got up on his knees and fumbled with his pajamas.

The next thing we heard was, "I can't see," as Bob turned on the dome light that was over his head.

Our car was suddenly transformed into a beacon of light in the darkened drive-in, with little Bob outlined in a halo of bright light for the world to see, peeing in a milk carton.

Dad yelled as he turned around and Mom was aghast at how her plan descended into utter chaos and public embarrassment. Horns started honking around us and we could hear people chuckling. Dad flipped off the dome light, putting an end to the show. Bob was flustered and missed the carton. Another fun night out with the kids.

—⁓—

One sunny Saturday afternoon, Mom decided that we should have McDonald's hamburgers for dinner. Now this was a treat beyond compare; we never ate McDonald's hamburgers at home.

We were all very excited, clapping our hands and jumping up and down singing a chorus of "Yes! Yes!"

But how was this going to happen? Dad was working overnight at the fire station and had taken the car.

Suddenly this whole idea of eating burgers and French fries at home seemed a little far-fetched. How would we get to McDonald's to get the food?

I should have given Mom more credit; she had a plan. She handed me a five-dollar bill from her wallet and told Ken and me to ride our bikes to the Pasadena Street McDonald's, buy the burgers and fries and hurry home so we could all eat around the table.

What a great idea! No one mentioned the fact that the only McDonald's was over five miles away. No big deal. Ken and I could find it on our trusty bikes.

Mom warned us not to eat any of the food until we got home and to be sure to bring her the change. She also said as a passing thought, to be careful, but to hurry home before the food got cold. She was thinking that she might have to warm the burgers up in the oven.

Ken and I hurried out the back door, grabbed the handlebars of our bikes, kicked up the stands, and pushed off down the driveway. The excitement of going to get dinner for the family propelled us forward at a rather fast pace.

After about a mile, we slowed down to a leisurely but steady pace heading west. We had a long way to go. Ken was always better at directions than I was and he took the lead, heading down streets we had never before traveled on.

We rode down one country-like dirt road that had a row of tall pine trees on one side and high steel towers carrying power lines on the other. The houses were spaced farther and farther apart. We came to the end of that road and Ken said we needed to turn left so we did.

After about another fifteen minutes of riding, we came to Clio Road, a very busy four-lane highway. We kept veering left and pedaling until we saw the golden arches off in the distance, standing out above the businesses and traffic. We made it!

Now the McDonald's we had back then were not like today's restaurants. There was no drive-thru, no dining room, and no playground.

The menus were very simple; cheeseburger, twenty cents; hamburger, fifteen cents; French fries, ten cents; and Coca-Cola drinks.

The building was a small square box with a large glass window across the front and a walk-up counter to order from. We parked our bikes and went up to the window. The young man behind the counter greeted us and we ordered what turned out to be four bags of burgers and fries. We paid him and I stuffed the dollars and small change into my pocket. We divided up the bags and headed home.

The ride home seemed to take forever. I was tortured by the mouth-watering smell of those French fries wafting back over the handlebars from the warm bags. It took all of my will power not to eat my portion on the way home. I'm sure Ken felt the same.

Mom had the table set when we finally got home and she put the food out for everyone to eat. We had a wonderful dinner and Ken and I felt proud that we were able to go and get it.

I'd never thought about it before, but I am sure it gave my mom a sense of accomplishment to provide that dinner without having a car. She was stuck at home because we only had one car growing up and it was Dad's transportation.

—⟋⟍⟍—

Our bikes took us everywhere. The surrounding streets and alleys were our domain and we knew them like the back of our hand.

One summer, a construction project was started on the block adjacent to ours and directly across from the deserted amusement park. A big power shovel was digging a deep basement for a new funeral home. This was the newest building to date to go up in our neighborhood.

We watched as the shovel filled the waiting dump trucks with loose dirt. Once a truck was loaded, it simply drove across the street to our block and dumped the dirt in the large vacant end lot that ran across the entire block.

Dumping like this happened all the time because no one seemed to care. Large dump trucks from the auto foundry dumped their loads of sand used in the casting process of car engines in the deserted amusement park.

We dug through those piles to pick out the unbroken lumps of hardened sand cores and we carved skulls from them. So no one thought anything was amiss as the trucks dumped the dirt from the new funeral home in the vacant lots across the street.

Mr. Branson opened his funeral home that year and I guess it was a success. I remember two things about him. First, he had twin daughters that were pretty cute but seemed a little stuck up. Probably because they were older than we were.

Second, and most importantly, by dumping the dirt from the excavation of his basement onto the end lot on our block, he unwittingly created an historical landmark that was known to all the neighborhood kids as simply "The Hills."

These contiguous piles of dumped dirt formed a formidable chain of mountains that started at the sidewalk of Winthrop Street. The Hills meandered east in an unbroken chain of peaks and valleys, connected by a single bike trail that threaded and twisted across the dizzying heights of the crest.

Okay, so with our fertile imaginations we saw something special in those neglected and unsightly hills. We played on their peaks for hours on end in almost any weather and every season. In the winter, we climbed the Alps and delivered messages to Army generals, only to get picked off by snipers and roll down the slope. In the summer, we rode our bikes at breakneck speeds across the razor thin trail running along the crest. With the wind in our faces and a devil-may-care attitude, we felt fairly invincible.

The trail ended in a long lazy slope down to a path that wiggled through the weeds and ended across from Frank's corner grocery store. Frank's was a small, family-run store with the world's largest candy counter next to the cash register. Dad would go to Frank's whenever he needed grown-up provisions like beer or baloney.

Whenever we found an empty pop bottle, we headed to Frank's and cashed it in for the two-cent deposit. We spent countless two-cent deposits at Frank's candy counter. Back then, two cents could buy a penny Bazooka bubble gum and two-for-one penny candies, like Mary Janes or Bit-O-Honeys.

One day, when I was around five years old, Mom sent me to Frank's with some money and a note. Frank filled a grocery bag with the requested items and he put the change in the bag.

I started home. I was supposed to be walking on the sidewalk; instead, I walked in the street along the curb, kicking stones.

Suddenly, I kicked at a stone and missed it. My foot stuck on something and I fell forward. I hit face-first on the steel cover of the sewer drain that was in the curbing. I don't remember much after that, except I walked home crying, and there was blood was all over the grocery bag.

I came in the kitchen and my mother screamed.

Her reaction scared me and I cried harder. I didn't know it, but my permanent front tooth had been knocked out and was dangling by the root from my mouth.

Dad was at the fire station and Mom was alone with me. She tried to calm me down as she quickly called Dad. I remember hearing him tell her over the phone to gently push the tooth back in, and hold it in place with a wet washcloth.

My dad arrived shortly after the call and we rushed to the hospital. The only thing I remember from the hospital is sitting on a table with several people dressed in white standing around me.

I couldn't see their faces; I could only see their white gowns.

They kept asking me over and over again, "Did your father hit you? It's okay, you can tell us."

I remember sobbing, and saying, "No, I fell in the gutter and hit my face!" I kept answering their repeated questions with the same line. I was scared, and thought, "Why don't they believe me?"

Next, I was sitting in an office with Mom and Dad and a very nice doctor dressed in a white gown. He was telling them that they were able to push the tooth back in place and so far, things seemed good.

My parents looked scared and happy at the same time. He told Mom that I could have as many Popsicles as I wanted, and I was to gently bite on the wooden Popsicle sticks. This would help keep my tooth in place and allow for healing.

When we got home, I got into my pajamas and Mom put me to bed on the living room couch and gave me a Popsicle. I lived on Popsicles and poached eggs on toast for a while.

Thanks to Mom and Dad's quick thinking, both my tooth and my devilish grin were saved that day.

—◇◇◇—

Several months after my front tooth had healed, Mom took Ken and me to our family dentist for the first time. Walking through his front door, we had no idea what to expect.

Dr. Bradley greeted us gruffly in his slightly wrinkled white lab coat. He had a big bushy mustache, black-framed glasses, and thick fingers. He lived and worked out of his dark-colored clapboard house across from North Flint Plaza. The narrow entrance hallway served as his waiting room. There were several well-worn chairs lined up against the wall and a small end table with a few dog-eared magazines. The door leading to the examination room was on the opposite side of the cramped hallway.

Being older, I went in first while Ken settled down with a magazine. Dr. Bradley sat me in a big, black, swivel chair with thick, padded arms and a headrest. I was too little to reach the headrest, so I scooted back the best I could and studied my surroundings.

I immediately saw a large, stork-like machine with a jointed arm. Black cables ran on tiny pulleys along both sides of the arm and connected to a gadget that looked like a drill—a much smaller version of the drills I'd seen my dad use. I had heard from kids at school that dentists used drills and thought this must be it. There was a large lamp directly overhead, a small sink gurgling on my left, and lots of little sharp picks and shiny tools all arranged on a white cloth-covered tray.

While I was taking in all these strange sights and sounds, Mom explained to the dentist that this was my first visit. They talked a bit and then she went out to keep Ken company.

Dr. Bradley moved the light and told me to open my mouth. He peered inside, poked around, mumbled to himself, and gave me precise instructions: sit up; open wider; turn this way; turn the other way.

After just a few minutes, he was finished. Hey, this wasn't so bad!

I thought I was all done and was prepared to hop down.

Mom appeared in the doorway, and Dr. Bradley reported, "He has five cavities. I can fill them all today. Is that okay?"

Mom nodded that it was, and then he asked, "Do you want him to have novocaine?"

"Is that extra?" Mom asked.

"Yes. Five dollars," he replied.

Mom did not have the extra money, so she reluctantly turned down the novocaine. Questions rolled around in my head. What's a cavity? What is novocaine? The answers would come soon enough as the dentist reached for his drill.

Dr. Bradley drilled and filled all five of my cavities that day. He kept telling me to hold still and to keep my mouth open. As the drill whined, I felt the vibration of the bit as it bored into each tooth. Was that smoke I smelled?! I yelled and gagged and squirmed for what seemed like an eternity.

At last, he hung up the drill and muttered that the worst part was over. For both of us. Next, he mixed up some silvery stuff (it was amalgam) and started to fill my cavities. No longer yelling, I just gulped deep breaths of relief.

When he was finished, I slid out of the chair and scurried back to the waiting room. Ken had a very strange look on his face. I must have been quite a sight, all red-faced and ragged.

Dr. Bradley looked over at Ken.

"You're next," he sighed.

Ken disappeared into the office. A brief conference with Mom followed, and then I heard Ken yelling.

As you can well imagine, it took me a very long time to get over my fear of going to a dentist.

—⁓—

Our living room was a small, rectangular box. In the farthest corner from the door and across from the couch, sat our Zenith black and white television set. It consisted of an oval screen with straight sides that was nestled in a big, blonde cabinet.

Our living room. Left to right: Bob, Ken, Mike holding toddler Don, and John posing as the Thinker.

The TV screen was a giant cathode-ray tube that took up most of the cabinet. Under the screen in the front of the cabinet, the speakers were hidden behind a brown mesh rectangle. The back of the cabinet was open for easy access to the tube tray that held the small four-to-six-inch tubes.

These tubes were made of glass and looked like long, skinny light bulbs with glowing filaments inside. We had a TV antenna that Dad had installed on top of the roof. The antenna was connected by cable to the back of the set to get reception.

The early TVs were very undependable. The screen would go blank in the middle of a show a couple of times a month. When this happened, Dad got up from the couch and hit the side of the cabinet with the palm of his hand. If that didn't solve the problem, he pulled the cabinet out from the corner so he could check the small tubes.

They glowed like light bulbs when they were working properly. Sometimes it was easy to see which tube was burned out because there was a black, smoky residue smeared on the inside of the glass tube. Most times, however, he couldn't tell.

Dad methodically took out the tubes he thought were bad and went to Cunningham's drug store to use their tube-testing stand. One at a time, he slipped his tubes into the testing receptacle. If the tube lit up, it was good, if not, it was bad.

After testing his tubes, he bought the appropriate replacements and returned home. He installed the tubes, fiddled with the controls, and when the picture was restored, pushed the cabinet back into the corner. Most of the time, he got the set working again. If not, he'd have to call the TV repairman.

—ɯ—

The evening television shows of the late 1950s were geared for adults. These shows were broadcast live and the actors had one chance to get it right. The early shows were comedy, singing, and mini-dramas. The screen was home to Milton Berle, George Gobel, Red Skelton, and Jackie Gleason, to name a few.

My dad sat on the couch at night, smoking a cigarette, drinking a beer, and laughing at the antics on the screen. Ken and I watched sometimes, but mostly we played with our trucks and cars.

Every spring we all awaited with great anticipation the special broadcast of a feature-length movie on TV. That movie was none other than *The Wizard of Oz*.

On the appointed evening, Mom popped popcorn and made Kool-Aid in the green thermos jug. We got into our pajamas and gathered in a semi-circle around the TV, waiting. Dad and Mom settled in on the couch.

The show started with a word from the show's sponsor, Kraft. The Kraft Company had the best commercials, highlighting their cheeses and latest products. We licked our lips and murmured, as black and white pictures of cheese rotated in front of our eyes. We could almost taste and smell the cheese. To this day, when I see *The Wizard of Oz*, I think of Kraft.

We watched the entire show in black and white. It would be several years before we discovered that the last half of the show was in color because we didn't have a color television.

The tornado scene was terrifying. The drama started when Dorothy left the old man's wagon under the wooden bridge to go home. We heard the wind picking up as the leaves and branches swayed wildly.

The old man clutched his horse's reins to his chest, and looking up at the darkening clouds, he said to his horse, "It's going to be a whopper." He then looked in the direction where Dorothy had gone and said, "I do hope she gets home."

We all somehow knew that she wouldn't.

We held our breath and watched through squinting eyes as Dorothy struggled against the howling wind, attempting to get home safely.

We bounced up and down on our little bent knees, making sobbing noises as we yelled, "Run!" at the TV screen to encourage Dorothy.

She couldn't hear us! The twister loomed big and powerful in the background behind the little farmhouse. The sinister, whirling, black funnel threw up massive dust clouds as it engulfed everything in its path.

We almost fainted as Dorothy stopped to pick up her suitcase and then her little dog, Toto, while trying to keep from being blown away.

Again, we yelled at the screen, "Leave it! Run!"

Again, she couldn't hear us.

I was really breathing hard now, eyes glued to the TV screen, mumbling words of encouragement over and over.

Suddenly the unthinkable happened; the adults were all going down into the backyard underground cellar!

The twister was so big and close that we couldn't hear anything but its loud roaring. It filled the screen behind them, tearing up the barnyard!

Aunty Em kept calling to Dorothy as Uncle Henry pulled Em into the shelter and the big wooden door banged shut!

I couldn't believe it! Dorothy was inside the house heading for the shelter when they closed the door. She yelled and stomped her foot on the big wooden door, but it remained firmly closed.

We could barely hear her cries over the noise of the twister. She ran back into the house, was hit on the head by a window frame, and blacked out.

Kraft was a very smart advertiser. They knew we needed a break after all this excitement. The screen shifted to a commercial shot of Kraft Parmesan cheese.

We ran to use the bathroom. When you are little boys, you can squeeze three around the toilet at once. The rest of the movie was very exciting. The other scary parts for me were the flying monkeys and Dorothy's group entering the witch's castle to get her broom.

The music that accompanied the guards as they hummed in deep, throaty voices was pretty unsettling. This was by far the best movie we had ever seen! We looked forward to its annual showing in our living room, made possible by Kraft.

—◠◡◠—

Uncle Bob was the first we knew to get a color television set. He worked at the Buick automobile factory and he seemed to have all the newest gadgets.

He bought a new Buick every year (he drank a lot and smashed up his cars) and he had an in-ground swimming pool in the backyard. He lived over on Philadelphia Street about three blocks from us with his wife, Lale, who was Mom's sister. They had one son, Jerry, who was a couple of years older than me.

One Sunday afternoon, Mom announced we were going over to Uncle Bob's that evening to watch *Walt Disney's Wonderful World of Color* on his brand new color TV.

She also threatened us, "Be good, or else."

Wow! We were going to watch *Disney* on Uncle Bob's new color TV! We could hardly wait. At the appointed hour, we got into our pajamas and loaded up the car with the popcorn bag and Kool-Aid jug. The short ride to their house gave Mom another opportunity to remind us to behave ourselves, or else.

We arrived and settled into the living room. Uncle Bob gave Dad a beer and Aunt Lale visited with Mom. Jerry played with his Hubley telephone truck, effectively ignoring us kids. The big, shiny, new color TV sat prominently in the best corner of the living room.

We were impressed, but the show that was playing was in black and white. Where was the color? Uncle Bob explained to everyone, with an air of authority, that color was so new that only certain shows, like *Disney*, were broadcasting in color. The show would be on in a few minutes and we would see for ourselves. I didn't really care at this point because I had never seen a color TV show before. I didn't know what I was missing.

We all gathered around, the kids in pajamas seated in a semicircle in front of the set with the adults on the big couch behind us. We munched popcorn, sipped Kool-Aid, talked, and waited.

Suddenly Uncle Bob said, "Here it comes!"

The commotion stopped and we all looked at the screen. What I saw next has been seared into my memory forever. We saw the Magic Kingdom's famous castle, in black and white, standing in the background with Tinker Bell flying out in front of it. Tinker Bell hesitated for a millisecond, and then she waved her wand across the screen.

The most beautiful colors imaginable flew from her wand in a pixie dust rainbow, expanding outward and filling the screen. The rainbow turned everything it touched into vivid, vibrant colors that burst out at us like fireworks.

Everyone in the room drew in a sharp breath, and as we exhaled all you could hear was, "Oooohhh! Aaaahhh!"

What a start to a show! I was mesmerized. The whole *Disney* program was in color! Donald Duck was white, with yellow feet and an orange bill, topped off by his blue cap! Every character and background was in beautiful, eye-popping color. I don't remember eating my popcorn.

When the show was over, the screen converted to black and white. Mom and Dad thanked Uncle Bob and Aunt Lale and they started herding us toward the front door.

I was so excited about what we had just seen, I blurted out to Mom in front of Uncle Bob and Aunt Lale, "Mom! Can we come back next Sunday to watch *Disney* again?"

Uncle Bob chuckled as Mom smacked me on the back of the head and told me to get in the car. So much for a repeat performance.

—⁓—

We actually didn't watch television very much growing up. The full color world outside was infinitely more interesting than the black and white world conjured up by the tubes inside a TV cabinet. We did, however, enjoy Saturday morning cartoons like *Tom and Jerry*, *Road Runner*, *Clutch Cargo*, *Bugs Bunny*, and *Johnny Quest*, to name a few.

The evening shows were Dad's pick. We watched *Combat!* with actor Vic Morrow and told everyone he was related to us, but he wasn't. He played Sergeant Sanders and carried what we called a "Hollywood" Thompson machine gun. Vic's "Hollywood" gun had a 20-round magazine that never ran out of bullets, and never needed any extra ammo. He had the same guys in his squad every week. They never got killed, only wounded, and would return the following week.

The show also had a new recruit added to Sergeant Sander's squad each week, and this was the guy we knew would be dead by the end of the show.

The same few guys on every show played the Germans. They were always lousy shots. They ran out of ammo or their bolt-action rifles jammed whenever Sergeant Sanders ran to a new position.

One night we were watching the show, eating popcorn. Sergeant Sander's heroic squad of expert marksmen was picking off Germans as they poked their heads up from under rubble or behind a tree.

Suddenly, a German soldier wearing a big, gray, coal bucket helmet poked his head up over a wall. I knew this man! It was Uncle Allerd from Grandpa's farm!

Now, I was not stupid; I knew it wasn't really our Uncle Allerd, but he sure did resemble the German soldier.

Before thinking, I exclaimed, "Look, it's Uncle Allerd!"

My punishment was stunningly swift. Mom was up off the couch in a flash! She slapped me with her hand across the back of my head so hard I saw stars. My popcorn went flying and Ken and Bob yelped in shock as if they themselves had been smacked.

I heard Mom yell, "We were on the American side!"

There you have it. I should have realized that my humorous observation about Uncle Allerd's look-alike would not be appreciated. Although my mother's family was of German descent, they all served in the American Army in WWII.

Grandpa's oldest son, Gervase Klein, was a medic in Patton's

Third Army at the Battle of the Bulge. I remember seeing a picture of him taken somewhere overseas in his WWII Army uniform standing next to his medic's truck. His boots were muddy and his uniform well worn. He looked tired, but he smiled at the camera. I was proud of my uncle and his service.

—⟋⟋⟍—

On Sunday evenings we would watch *The Ed Sullivan Show*. This was a variety show with singers, performers, and comedians all introduced by Mr. Sullivan. The one show I remember was in the early 1960s when Ed introduced the Beatles to the world.

We were all seated in our regular watching positions as the warm-up acts came and went. Finally, Mr. Sullivan introduced the Beatles. The curtains opened and there they were: John, Paul, George, and Ringo! They were standing in a semi-circle centered on Ringo and his drums. They wore short, black, suit jackets, white shirts and slim black ties. Their black slacks partially covered pointed, black half boots.

They stood tall and looked at ease, each one sporting a casual smile. The crowning touch was their hair. They had hair! They wore their hair over their ears. Long but kempt. Stylish yet wild. Rough and suave at the same time.

The Beatles opened with "I Want to Hold Your Hand." The girls in the audience screamed and kept screaming. It was absolutely unreal, beautiful and cool! We were glued to the television. We loved them! Dad just kept mumbling about how awful their hair looked. Mom kept quiet. I think the hairdresser in her must've been running her fingers through that unruly hair.

—⟋⟋⟍—

The outdoor fun did not stop because of winter. We looked forward to the first snowfall with great anticipation. When you are small, the snow is always deep.

Walking to school in a snowstorm was work. Walking home from school in a snowstorm was exciting. We knew we'd soon be out shoveling sidewalks and building snow forts! If the snow was sticking, we built forts. Sometimes we placed small boards across the top of the snow walls and packed snow on top of the boards to make a roof.

We each had a sled that took the place of our bikes in the snow. We dragged them everywhere. I put my left foot on the back of my sled while holding the rope. Then I pushed the sled with my right foot, making "Giddy up" noises to encourage the imaginary team of horses pulling my imaginary wagon.

On our sleds, we toted some dried corn stalks we had gathered from Grandpa's farm; we pretended they were Davy Crockett rifles.

In our front yard, we shoveled a large circle and divided it into four pieces of pie. This was a tag game we created and named "Cut the Pie." The center spot was the free, safe space. On every other place along the paths, we were fair game to be tagged. Only one person at a time could rest on the free spot. If someone else was there first, the runner was forced back into the game.

We ran around the snow packed circle and across the pie legs chasing each other. It would get dark early and it was even more fun chasing each other around in the frozen snow under the streetlights. Mom would usually call us in just before dinner.

On Saturday afternoons when we had a lot of snow on the ground, Dad took us to Iroquois Hill to sled. We threw our sleds into the back of the station wagon and he drove us the three miles to the hill.

Iroquois Hill was located on the right hand side of DuPont Street, about a half-mile from Forest Park. The hill was situated between a large church and a private residence. Dad pulled into the church parking lot and dropped us off, telling us to be good.

Then he got in the car and drove away to take care of his errands. He always told us he would be back in a couple of hours, but since we didn't have watches, it made no difference to us.

We joined the crowd of kids and adults at the top of the hill and lined up for our first run of the day. This was a huge hill. The drop was about 90 feet, and the run from top to bottom where we stopped, took us over 150 feet down the hill.

We lined up and pushed off, stretched out on our stomachs to cut the air resistance and go faster. We steered left or right by pushing and pulling the front steering rod with our hands, just like on our bikes.

For about thirty seconds, we were flying! Once at the bottom, we grabbed our sled ropes and began the long trek back up the hill. The longer we stayed, the longer this trip took. By the time Dad came back to pick us up, we were cold and tired.

Ice-skating was the other wintertime activity we enjoyed. Ken and I each got a pair of hockey skates one year. We never did get the hang of using those skates.

Dad traded them in for figure skates and we immediately took to them. The figure skates had toe picks on the front blades that helped us stop, start, and turn by digging in or dragging them on the ice. Ken and I actually got pretty good at ice-skating.

On the other side of Forest Park, farther from our home, there was a large open area next to the main road that the City turned into an ice skating pond. They plowed the snow off the field and formed snow walls around the large rectangular skating arena. The Fire Department flooded the field, and the bitter cold temperatures did the rest. The next morning, the ice skating arena was ready for skaters.

The City Maintenance Department brought out a wooden shed with lights and a heater inside and parked it on the edge of the ice. We

Left to right: Ken, Bob, and Mike building a snow fort in our back yard. Our garage and cherry tree are to the immediate right behind Mike.

went inside to change into skates, warm up, change socks, or just take a break from the cold. They also set up floodlights around the outdoor arena and the side parking lot. On school nights, we could skate until ten p.m., and on Friday and Saturday nights, until midnight.

We spent a lot of time there and became very good skaters. Dad drove us and dropped us off, but when we were in eighth grade, we started walking to the arena.

The shortest route home was about two miles away if we cut through the Forest Park woods. It was always dark and we didn't dally. A few times I made the trip by myself. It was really spooky.

I learned how to play "Pom-Pom." Someone yelled "Pom-Pom" and everyone gathered in a group on a long side of the arena. The person who called the game was "it," and he stood in the center of the arena, facing the mob.

When he was ready, he yelled "Pom-Pom!"

The entire crowd raced across the ice, trying not to be tagged, and to reach the safety of the opposite side. The object of the game was for the person who was "it" to tag people as they attempted to cross. Once someone was caught, he joined the taggers in the center. It was harder to tag someone at first. Once a few kids were caught, the taggers in the middle quickly grew in number.

Finally, it got down to the best skater, left all alone on the side, looking at the mob in the middle.

The mob yelled, "Pom-Pom!" and it was all over. The game broke up and normal skating resumed. We made lots of friends while skating.

—w—

Dad's favorite pastime was to load us up in the car and go for a drive to look for deer. Mom and Dad never tired of this family routine.

We kids groaned whenever Dad said, "Ma, let's go for a little ride."

We protested and moaned, but in the end we all assembled in our places in the car. Mom rode up front (usually holding a baby) and the rest of us spread out across the back seat.

Mile after miserable mile we drove.

Every now and then, Mom sang out, "There's one!" or Dad

exclaimed, "Look, there are three of them!"

They never seemed to tire of this fun.

We dutifully chorused a half-hearted, "Hmmm" or mumbled a pathetic, "Wow."

Deer were not the only animals they found. During one such ride up North, we were in the 1955 Chevrolet sedan, driving down a dirt road with woods on either side of the car. It was dark outside; we could only see the road bordered by thick evergreen trees illuminated by the car's headlights.

Suddenly, there was a small bear cub right in the middle of the road, caught in the glare of the headlights. Dad stopped the car and the bear ran off into the woods.

Mom said, "Oh, Dick, go into the woods and bring the baby bear back so the kids can see it!" Now we all saw the bear; we didn't need to see it again.

Dad looked at her and said, "Are you crazy! I'm not going in there and run into the mother bear!"

Mom kept whining and asking Dad to go into the woods. He finally drove off and she was quiet.

Years later, Ken said with a chuckle, "She knew what she was doing."

—⟋⟋⟍—

One afternoon up near Selfridge Air Force Base, Dad stopped the car on a deserted dirt road by a large hill. At the top of the hill was a tall chain link fence that ran parallel with the road. There were signs attached to the fence with red warning letters, but they were too far away to read.

We started to climb the hill toward the fence; we figured Dad wanted us to read the signs. About half way up the grassy hill, we heard a loud, roaring noise. It was getting louder, and louder. It got very loud! We couldn't hear each other yelling. The ground shook!

Suddenly, the largest airplane I'd ever seen roared directly over our heads.

Dad and Mom were screaming something. Their mouths were

open but we couldn't hear them for the giant airplane thundering right over us.

We were at the end of a military runway and a B-52 Stratofortress Bomber was taking off. This bomber had a wingspan of 185 feet, weighed 92 tons and was propelled by eight jet engines. It was gargantuan!

We stood paralyzed, looking up with our mouths open. Dad finally broke the spell and quickly loaded us into the car to make our getaway before we were captured by the military police.

—⟋⟍⟋—

Dad had other favorite pastimes. During our rides in the country in the late summer, we were to be on the lookout for farmers that sold sweet corn by the roadside. When we found one, Dad stopped and the fun began.

Dad asked the farmer how much the corn was and the farmer told him, "Fifty cents a dozen."

Dad said, "I'll take a dozen."

If the farmer didn't give him thirteen ears of corn to make a baker's dozen, then the argument began. They haggled back and forth. In the end, Dad always got his thirteen ears of corn and we headed home with Dad whistling a happy tune as he drove.

Dad tried this tactic one time in the grocery store. He placed thirteen ears of corn on the conveyor belt and the clerk rang up and charged him for thirteen ears.

Dad dutifully explained that he always got a baker's dozen because there's always a rotten ear in the bunch.

The cashier and Dad argued loudly back and forth as people in line watched. Ken and I were embarrassed and we slumped down, trying to hide under the conveyor belt.

Dad finally played his trump card.

He proclaimed loudly with a flourish, "The farmer always gives me thirteen ears!"

The cashier looked astounded and said, "Then go get your corn from the farmer!"

Dad sheepishly paid for the thirteen ears and we left the store. It was a quiet ride home.

—⟶

I remember going with Ken and Dad one beautiful fall day to a local cider mill in the country. The building was a long, low wooden structure that was painted green. It had a long wooden counter where they sold bags of apples and glass gallon jugs of apple cider. The aroma of pressed apples hung in the air like perfume.

The apple press was on one end of the building where we watched them press the apples. Glass jugs were sitting at the bottom of the press waiting to be filled with the golden juice. There were a lot of flies buzzing around. Yellow sticky strings of flypaper covered with dead flies hung from the ceiling.

Dad always got a bag or two of Macintosh apples and a gallon of cider. They also sold cider doughnuts and we each got a hot one, fresh out of the fryer. They smelled heavenly and tasted even better.

—⟶

Dad was famous for his bargain-hunting. One time, he bought a ring of baloney from Frank's corner store. He came home, ground up half of it and mixed it with sweet pickles and Miracle Whip. He opened a loaf of Wonder bread and made sandwiches. We loved them and ate with gusto.

Dad ate two or three sandwiches. Shortly after, he was standing by the sink, holding his stomach.

He said to Mom, "I don't feel so good. I think that baloney was rotten."

She made the appropriate soothing mumbles as she dried dishes.

Dad said, "I'm returning that baloney to Frank's and getting my money back!"

Dad wrapped up the remaining half of the baloney and told Ken and me to get in the car. We drove the short distance to Frank's and went in the screen door.

Frank was behind the wooden counter reading a newspaper.

Dad walked up and said, "This baloney I bought from you is rotten. I want my money back."

Frank put down the paper, took the remainder of the baloney and looked at it carefully.

He finally looked at Dad and said, "Where's the other half?"

Dad said, "I ate it. How do you think I found out it was rotten?"

Now Ken and I were used to this kind of exchange between Dad and merchants, so as usual we made ourselves small.

Frank and Dad argued back and forth for several minutes until we heard, "No wonder you're sick. You stuffed your gut with half of the baloney and made yourself sick!"

Dad finally got half of his money back. He went out to the car whistling one of his trademark victory tunes.

—\\\—

One day, Ken and I tried to play a trick on Frank.

Well, come on. We had a good teacher!

The newspaper had a picture of a real one-dollar bill printed in color as part of an article on counterfeiting. We carefully cut out that dollar bill and headed to Frank's corner store.

We opened the screen door and a little bell jingled to announce our presence. We walked up to the counter and one of Frank's summer high school boys waited on us.

Like a couple of big spenders, we pointed at the candy saying, "I'll take one of those, and two of those, and some of that."

When we figured we had about a dollar's worth of candy piled up, the clerk rang it up. I coolly slid the fake dollar bill across the counter.

Everything stopped.

The young man just glared at us with sheer annoyance and yelled at us to get out of there.

We didn't wait to be told twice; we fled! Such was the abrupt end to our would-be crime spree with counterfeit currency.

Yes, our parents found out.

Yes, we were given a good spanking.

No, we never tried that stunt again.

CHAPTER FOUR

Jim LaVictoire was my best friend growing up. We met in first grade at St. Agnes School and shared classes all the way through high school, graduating together from St. Agnes in 1969. Jim was our senior class president. He lived about a mile away from me to the east of Flint Park.

We started visiting each other's houses once we had bikes and our freedom. We met to play on Saturdays during school and most every day in the summer.

When Jim was not around, I played with Tommy Montpas who lived two houses down and was a year older. This worked out fine until Tommy started eighth grade and football. We didn't get together too much after that.

Jim and I loved to explore the old abandoned amusement park and the swamp next to Devil's Lake. The whole area was overgrown with tall weeds and bushes. Most of the old wooden buildings were still standing.

Everything there was vandalized, not so much with graffiti, but mostly with deliberate, physical damage. Windows were broken and glass crunched under foot. Everything that was once considered useful was gone; leaving empty, broken shells covered by vines and faded paint.

At the far west edge of the park sat the old roller rink, still standing. It was a large, two-story wooden structure that had a massive, half-round domed roof.

Just beyond the old roller rink was the end of the amusement park and the beginning of the swamp. It was the buffer zone between Devil's Lake and the park. The swamp was a mystical playground that was covered by greenish water, and dotted with small earthen islands. The land supported weeds and flowering bushes that attracted swarms of hovering, blue-green dragonflies.

At the water's edge, there were long, brown reeds with fluffy tops that swayed gently in the summer breeze. In the shallow water, we could catch tadpoles, frogs, and even crawfish. We loved to wander through the park and end up at the swamp. All around were the sights and sounds of nature, from the buzzing of insects and the singing of birds, to the throaty thrumming of bullfrogs. We played and explored in this wonderland for hours on end.

One particular sunny day, Jim and I were having fun at the swamp when Jim stood still. He was standing at the edge of the water, looking toward the island that was in the middle of the swamp. This particular island was about thirty feet long by ten feet wide, covered with bushes and outlined with reeds. Jim's face was contorted, eyes squinting, and I could tell that he was deep in thought.

Suddenly, he declared, "I think we can cross over to that island."

I was a bit surprised and said, "How are we going to do that and not get wet?"

The island was at least fifteen feet from where we stood on the dry bank, and the water looked pretty deep.

Jim said with confidence, "I have a plan. It is my Universal Plan."

Jim explained that we needed long lengths of boards. This part of the plan was fairly easy; the old amusement park was right next door and it was loaded with old, used lumber. We gathered several long boards and dragged them back to the water's edge.

There was a small earthen mound showing above the water between the island and our shore. It was almost exactly in the middle. Jim explained that we needed to drop the first long board so it would land on this dirt mound. I was starting to get a glimpse of the bigger picture, and it didn't look good.

We stood the first long board up on the edge of our shore. Jim spent several seconds eyeing the middle mound and adjusting the position of the standing board. The board was about ten feet long and a foot wide. It was starting to get heavy.

Finally, Jim said, "Let go, I have it!"

I released my grip, and Jim gave the board a measured, gentle push toward the water. The board started to fall. Slowly at first, then gaining speed quickly, it reached the halfway point over the water.

There was a loud Splash! followed immediately by a dull Thud! Water sprayed into the air in the form of a "V" away from both sides of the board. The plank quivered slightly in the disturbed water. Jim turned to me with a big smile. The plank had hit the mound in the middle of the swamp, and it held.

Okay, I was impressed. Jim spent the next few minutes walking along the shore, looking at the board from different angles. He announced that we were ready for the next step in his Universal Plan.

Jim said that he was going to cross over on the plank to the dirt mound. Once he was in place, it would be my job to hand him the next board. He would then place the last section of the bridge, stretching from the mound to the island. I have to say that, so far, I was impressed with his skill and determination, although I was a little more skeptical about this next part.

Jim walked very carefully on his bridge across the water. He held his arms straight out from his sides, wobbling with every step, just like the circus high-wire performers did way up under the circus tent. I held my breath. About halfway over, he almost fell, but he regained his balance and continued on.

When his feet were firmly on the earth mound at the end of the board, he turned around and waved. I picked up the next board and moved into position at the edge of the water. The board was heavy, so I laid it on top of the first board and started to push it toward Jim. It got caught a couple of times, but I was able to free it by twisting it. I continued to push the board until Jim had a good hold on it.

The next part of Jim's Universal Plan was the hardest. He had to maneuver the board by himself, since the mound only had room for one. He grunted and groaned as he hefted the board up from a flat position to vertical. He baby-stepped in a circle on the mound, with the board standing upright, until he was in position to drop it. He aimed the best he could and dropped the second board toward the island. It hit the shore of the island with a thud and a spray of water. So far, the plan was working perfectly.

Once the board was in place, Jim started to move along it toward the island. Suddenly, he slipped and lost his balance. He went over, arms flailing like a windmill, and headed for the water.

At the last moment, he managed to put his leg out so that he landed standing up. The water was up to his knees. The bridge was gone. He walked back to shore through the muck. What a mess. He cleaned up the best he could and we headed home. To this day, we still crack a smile when we talk about the Universal Plan.

—⁓—

One day we were exploring in the old roller rink. We had to be very careful not to step on rusty nails as we picked our way over piles of old broken boards, glass, and crumpled paper. We made it to the roof and were sitting on the top looking over the park.

We saw a group of kids playing near the front of the park. Suddenly a police car appeared and stopped the kids. We dropped down behind the top curve of the roof and watched as the police called the kids over and talked to them, probably telling them they could not be there.

Suddenly, the loudspeaker on top of the police car boomed out in a very authoritarian voice, "You two on the roof. Come down and come over here!"

We were terrified. If they told our parents, we would be in big trouble!

We scrambled down, keeping the building between the police car and us. We hit the bottom and decided to run for it. If we could go into the park and hide, we figured they would tire of searching for us and go away.

We took off running down the old circle park road that was now just barely an outline, overgrown with weeds and strewn with junk.

We got about half a mile away when we saw the police car coming slowly down the circle. The tires made crunching noises on the broken glass and you could see the weeds being pushed out of the way as if a giant monster was stalking us through the tall grass.

The loudspeaker blared, "You two, come out! Come over here!"

We were breathing very hard and Jim looked a little funny. We ran about another quarter of a mile and the car was still back there, slowly making its way through the park. We could barely get a glimpse of it through the trees and tall grass. They were not quitting.

Unexpectedly, Jim sat down on a box by the side of the road.

I yelled, "What are you doing? Come on, we gotta keep moving!"

Jim was pretty winded and said, "No, I'm going to sit here. They won't know it was me up there."

I looked at him to see if he was kidding and said, "Are you nuts?"

But he did not want to move and the car was getting closer. At any minute they would see us.

In a flash, I saw a group of boys playing guns over by the place where trucks from the Buick Foundry dumped slag sand from their engine molds. Among the group, I could make out our good buddy Larry Morgan and my brother Ken.

I grabbed Jim and pulled him up, explaining as we ran over to the group. Jim and I picked up sticks and started shooting bad guys with the gang. About thirty seconds later, the police car came by and one of the officers asked if we had seen two big kids running this way.

Larry said, "No." Everyone was making a big racket shooting and playing.

The police thanked us and left the park. Jim and I heaved a huge sigh of relief.

—⟋∿⟍—

Jim and I did some pretty crazy things together growing up. He liked to play with matches. Through the grace of God, he never was injured or burned anything down (except for the tree in his front yard), but he sure was drawn to the flame. About the most he would do was to start a few small fires and put them out. This was dangerous and we both knew better, but we were kids and we thought we knew everything about everything.

One day, the doghouse in his back yard burned down—the dog was not in it. It was an open and shut case. Jim was blamed, found guilty, and punished by his parents.

Jim professed his innocence throughout his entire life, but to no avail. He did have a little bit of a rap sheet, after all.

At his sixtieth birthday party, Jim's older brother, Joe, stood up in front of everyone and said, "I think the statute of limitations has expired; I would like to make a confession. Jim did not burn down the dog house. I did."

Jim was stunned. Everyone laughed and howled. All these years, Jim had been blamed for burning down the doghouse, and he really didn't do it. Like a man falsely imprisoned, Jim was finally vindicated and set free. He and Joe hugged.

One day, Jim wanted to buy some matches because we were going to the park. We decided not to go to Frank's corner store. Everyone in the store knew us and knew our parents, so we couldn't go there to buy our matches. We decided to go to the other little corner store on the other side of the park. This store was called Ziddo's and was run by an Italian family. They didn't know us.

We walked in and slowly went up to the wooden counter.

Mr. Ziddo was behind the counter in a white apron, wiping his hands on a towel. He smiled at us and said, "Can I help you boys?"

We looked up at him as he stared at us. I was nervous.

With one finger, Jim slid a penny across the counter toward him and said, "My mother sent me to get a book of matches for her."

Mr. Ziddo stopped wiping his hands and looked at the penny for what seemed like a very long time.

Suddenly he threw his arms up in the air, and waving the towel over our heads, he screamed, "Get out of here!"

I almost fainted! We must have looked like the two stooges, each trying to get out the screen door in front of the other one. We didn't stop running until we were back on our side of the park.

I told Jim through gasps and wheezes, "Forget the matches." We just went and played in the park instead.

Mr. Ziddo probably tells the story of how he scared two kids out of their wits that day and kept them from who knows what kind of trouble. In our tight-knit community, most grown-ups could be counted on to keep an eye on the neighborhood kids—an informal system of checks and balances.

—ᏤᏤ—

One evening, Jim and I were walking through the old amusement park. The park was halfway between our homes. We were about to go our separate ways when Jim saw a couple of newly excavated holes in the ground and we went over to investigate.

The holes had been dug by a big power shovel. They would become basements for new homes that were going up near the east edge of the park. We walked over and looked down into the first pit. It was a big, dark hole with vertical sides about twelve feet deep.

Jim said, "Let's go down there."

I wasn't so sure about that idea; it was late and we needed to be home. Jim kept insisting and the next thing I knew, we were both jumping down into the pit.

I remember hitting the bottom and rolling over.

I heard Jim cry out, "I can't move my foot, and it hurts!"

After a quick look we surmised that Jim's ankle was broken. He was in some pain and moaning a little. I looked up at the sides of the pit. They were straight up, with no way to climb out. Overhead, the stars twinkled in the blue-black sky.

We were in a deep, dark pit in a deserted amusement park at night, and no one could hear our pitiful cries for help. We tried yelling for help anyway, unsuccessfully. I needed to get Jim out or go find help.

Maybe it was the adrenaline, but my creative problem solving kicked in and I had an idea. I dug some hand and foot holds in the wall with my hands and was able to climb out, carrying Jim as he helped with his arms and good leg. We collapsed on top, panting, and rested. I helped him hobble home and turned him over to his mother who always seemed to be waiting for us. It could have been so much worse.

—ᏤᏤ—

One summer evening, I was enjoying a game of kickball under the streetlights at our intersection. We used the sewer grates at each corner as bases and the manhole cover in the middle was the pitcher's mound.

The pitcher rolled a large ball toward home base. The runner kicked the ball and ran to first base or maybe even second. The other team caught the ball and threw it. If the ball hit him between bases, he was out. The only breaks we took were to let cars drive through.

Our house was second from the corner and we kept playing kickball until Mom yelled from the front door to come home. I never left the game before she yelled, but this night, something was different.

Right in the middle of the game, I had the urge to go home. I said good night to my friends and started walking. I didn't know why I was leaving. I just knew I had to go home right then.

When I walked in the front door, Mom was sitting on the couch, holding baby Mary and screaming hysterically. My brother John, about three, was sitting on the floor with our little brother, Don.

Don was choking!

Don standing behind our house next to our 1960 Chevrolet station wagon.

His face was purple and his eyes were bulging; he looked terrified. John was crying and there were marbles all around them.

I ran over and grabbed Don by the ankles. I hoisted him up and gave him a hefty slap on the back. Suddenly a blue marble and a lot of green mucus flew out of his mouth.

I heard a huge intake of air as he gulped greedily at life. Mom picked him up and rocked him and I helped clean up the mess and threw away the marbles.

Don says he remembers that night, and every so often, I get a note or he reminds me of how I saved his life. He vividly recalls popping the marble into his mouth and that immediately he could not breathe.

He says he remembers everyone crying and Mom screaming. He couldn't talk and everything was going black. He felt me scoop him up and hit him on the back, and he says that intake of air after the marble popped out was like a miracle.

I'm so glad I was there and able to act. I realize that it wasn't that I wanted to go home that night; it was God directing me, and I'm ever so grateful that I listened.

Mike in front. Left to right in back: Bob and Ken with Dad holding John. Taken on our back steps before the addition Dad built.

CHAPTER FIVE

If you ask Ken or me what our favorite part of summer was, it was the time in late July or early August when we went up North to Aunt Francis' cottage. Dad's eldest sister had a little square cottage on Elk Lake near West Branch. Every year, she gave her brothers and sisters and their families a week in the cottage as a gift. What a joy it was to go on vacation to the lake!

Getting ready to go up North on vacation was always a time of anticipation. Dad loaded the car as Mom pulled together clothes, food, and baby items. Seems Mom always had a baby in her care. Finally the moment arrived when the car was packed. We climbed in and headed

Mike, front left, Ken, and friends playing in the sandbox at Aunt Francis' cottage.

out the driveway, leaving our home life behind for a little while.

Ken and I watched the road, anxiously looking for the landmarks that told us we were getting close. Dad always stopped for gas and cheese in Pinconning, a little town well-known for its cheese.

Dad went into the shop and asked the man to slice off sections of cheese from big cheese wheels and package them up in white waxed paper. The heavenly aroma of so many cheeses and hard sausages wafted throughout the shop, making our little tummies rumble.

Dad paid the man and loaded the cheese in the car. He always gave us a slice and he and Mom shared a piece for the road.

At the gas station, Dad picked out several long cane poles for fishing at the lake and tied them to the top of the car. These bamboo poles stood in a big barrel next to the pump, looking like giant stalks of dry grass gently rattling in the breeze.

Once at the lake, we tied on some fishing line, added a hook and a bobber, and our poles were ready. Under logs, we found worms to bait the hooks then waded out into the lake in our swimming trunks to the end of the green dock. We'd catch bluegills and little sunfish. We stayed out all day playing in the lake and woods.

There were lots of fun things to do at the cottage; we were never

Mike displaying the 12-inch bass he caught at Elk Lake while fishing in the boat with Dad. Ken is on the left, John in front and Mom, far left, sitting on the dock.

bored. I liked to play with my Army men and trucks. I sat somewhere along the path going down to the lake, and created Army bases, cut roads in the grass, and drove my trucks in the sand.

I could play for hours with my toys but the best fun was shooting my Daisy pump BB gun. I had wanted a BB gun for the longest time, and just like in the movie, *A Christmas Story*, my mom said I'd shoot my eye out, or worse yet, one of my brothers' eyes!

Just like Ralphie, it was an uphill battle convincing Dad to buy me one. I tried every angle, and like Ralphie, I always came up empty.

One summer, we loaded up the station wagon, ready to go on vacation. Mom was up front holding a baby, and Ken and Bob and I were in the back seat.

I was feeling a little down because I had asked Dad again a couple of days earlier if I could please have a BB gun. No luck.

He said, "No."

Dad locked the back door of the house and slipped into the car. He turned around asked if we had packed everything.

We all answered in chorus, "Yes."

We were a little bored and impatient because this was probably the tenth time he'd asked us.

He said, "Michael, why don't you reach over the back seat and see if my fishing rod is there."

I knew it was because I had seen it, and I said so.

He said, "Reach over the back seat and see."

I huffed a little as I reached back blindly over the seat until my fingers came in contact with something cool, metallic, and smooth.

Dad saw my face and said, "Go ahead and pull it up." I wrapped my hand around the steel barrel and pulled up a Daisy pump BB gun! And it was loaded!

Those little copper BBs rolled up and down inside the barrel as I tilted the gun, making a noise that I never forgot. To this day, when I hear BBs rolling in a gun barrel, it takes me back to that day and all the fun I had up North.

I clumsily pulled the gun over my head and probably pointed it at everyone in the car.

Mom yelled at me and told Dad, "Make him put that thing away!"
Ken said, "Wow!"

Struggling to grasp the importance of the moment, my little brother
Bob fell silent.

We were in the car facing out the driveway and Dad said, "Go
ahead and give it a try."

I stuck the barrel out the window, pumped the slide on the second
try, and pulled the trigger.

Ping!

The BB hit Mr. Whitaker's house next door, ricocheting noisily off
of his aluminum siding.

Dad said, "Okay, that's enough. Just be careful with that gun."

End of safety briefing. I placed the gun in the back of the car and
realized just how long this trip would be! That BB gun was my constant companion up North from that day on.

—⟋⟍⟍—

Ken and I spent almost our entire time up North outside. In the
mornings after a bowl of cereal, we were out and about exploring
around the cottage and across the dirt road in the woods, looking for
snakes and other wildlife. I always carried my BB gun "locked and
loaded," ready to shoot any varmint. Birds were always a favorite target back then, but they didn't have to worry. I was a lousy shot.

Mom yelled for us to come in for lunch around noon. After Velveeta
grilled cheese sandwiches and a bowl of tomato soup, we were ready
to hit the screen door again.

As soon as lunch was finished, we pestered Mom to let us go
swimming. Jumping into our swimsuits, we hit the beach! The cottage
fronted right on Elk Lake.

To get to the water, we ran down the well-worn sand trail that
started at the front door and curled around the right side of the big
screened-in porch by the sand box. We gathered steam as we ran, following the zigs and zags down the big hill to the beach.

The water always seemed to be shining, green-blue, and shimmer-
ing. The little green wooden dock poked out from the shore into the

lake. The water was waist deep until we got about five feet from the end of the dock, then the green-blue color turned a deep, dark blue-black as the sandy bottom immediately dropped off, giving way to murky depths.

Ken and I had taken swimming lessons at Haskell Community Pool near our home in Flint, but we always wore the orange floatation life vests from Dad's boat when swimming in the deep water. We swam, floated, and played "Torpedoes away!" for what seemed like hours, but in reality, it was usually just until Mom got tired of sitting on the shore watching us.

Early every morning and late in the afternoon, Dad took the aluminum rowboat out on the lake and went fishing. He could sit for hours in that boat and drown worms. He kept the big fish he caught and placed them in an old wooden live trap that was near our dock.

After fishing, he'd head over to the tavern at the end of the road for some beers.

One day, he caught a really big monster bass. He was so excited! He immediately came in from the lake and showed us his catch.

He then carefully put it in the live trap and went to the tavern. As the story goes, he told everyone who would listen about the record-

Dad holding John as Ken and Mike attempt to stuff him into the fishing net while Bob grins for the camera.

breaking bass that he had caught. I am sure, as with all good fishing tales involving massive quantities of beer, the bass got bigger with each telling.

Dad came home late that night and went to bed. The next morning, to his dismay, he discovered that his trophy bass was gone from the live trap! The investigation began.

Someone had to have come by late at night and stolen the bass from the trap. There was no other explanation we could conjure up that made sense to him. Someone had stolen his record-breaking bass.

The favorite theory was that some dirty rascal from the tavern came by in his boat that night after my dad had gone to bed and stole his fish.

He even swore he had heard a motorboat sneaking by our shore as he drifted off to sleep.

He never solved the mystery of the missing bass; and try as he might, he never caught another one as big. I think the whole episode soured him as he thought of thieves infiltrating up North.

—𝍢—

One sunny day, Ken and I were exploring down near the water and

Dad showing Mike how to row the boat. Dad loved to fish and spent a lot of time in that boat catching the big ones.

Mike in the water fishing with a cane pole, Ken holding a bluegill, and Bob in the Army hat next to our up North friends.

we found a big, brownish-tan, teardrop-shaped "basketball" hanging from a tree branch on the lot next door. We watched it for a while and saw what we thought were honeybees flying around it.

I decided that it would be a good idea to fire a couple of well-aimed BBs into this thing and see what happened.

Ken was always a little more skeptical than I, and he said, "I don't think that would be a good idea, Mike."

I pooh-poohed his advice, raised my trusty shooting iron, took aim, and fired.

Nothing happened. I pumped another round into the chamber, aimed, and fired again. No one home. I raised the gun a third time and fired. I was shocked to see a cloud of hornets come bursting out of the hive, heading straight for us!

We ran for our lives! We were not too smart, because instead of running downhill toward the water, we ran uphill to the cottage. Big mistake. Running uphill is always harder and slower than running downhill.

We swatted and yelled as the lead scouts easily caught up to us. We were still swatting and yelling as we ran past the front of the cottage, headed down the dirt road. I can only imagine what Mom must

My brother John enjoying the water by the dock.

have thought as she watched us from the front screen door with a baby in her arms. Mom never drank alcohol, but not because we never gave her a good reason not to drink.

About thirty minutes later, we were again at the water's edge by our dock. We had managed to escape the hornets with only minor wounds. I decided that we needed to find targets that were easier than birds, safer than hornets, and couldn't fight back.

I had it! We would shoot crawfish!

After several failed attempts at shooting them in the water, I realized that the crawfish were too deep and the BBs lost their punch very quickly under the water.

I directed Ken to catch a big one. He very skillfully pulled up a dripping wet crawfish, careful not to get pinched by its claws.

I told him to place it on the dock and I stood over the captive, aiming my BB gun almost directly down at it. I was about to squeeze the trigger when something very odd happened.

I thought about safety! I reasoned that if I shot my BB gun at this downward angle on the dock, the BB would go right thru the crawfish, ricochet, and possibly hit me! This would never do.

I told Ken about my moment of safety brilliance.

He said, "Now you're talking."

I pondered the situation and decided that the safest, surest way to dispatch the critter was to lay the BB gun down on the dock and shoot the crawfish sideways. I also decided that the safest direction to shoot would be off the end of the dock and out toward the lake. I carefully lined up the shot and we waited as the crawfish crept toward the end of the barrel.

Hold it. Hold it. Almost there. Now! I pulled the trigger and heard that familiar Thump! The gun jumped, propelling the BB from the end of the barrel.

The little round copper ball hit the crawfish with a Thunk! It was followed by a very loud Pling! The BB traveled straight over the surface of the water and hit the side of Dad's aluminum boat.

He just happened to be out on the lake fishing. As safe as I thought I was in preparing this shot, I failed to look downrange to make sure the area was clear. Big mistake!

We looked up in horror as Dad waved his fist, screaming, "Hey, you little blankety-blanks!!"

We didn't wait to hear anything else. We took off running up the hill again. Dad stayed out in the boat, and if Mom saw what happened, she never said anything.

—ɷ—

Ken in the middle, sitting on a boat with two boys from up North.

Bob was shot twice as we were growing up. I was blamed and punished for both incidents, but I was only guilty of one.

One summer up North, I was playing with Tommy, a boy my age who lived up North all year long. We were on our dock, shooting our BB guns over the water. Tommy had a Red Ryder rifle.

We were having fun when Bob showed up. I don't know how old he was, but he was wearing a diaper and holding his teddy bear.

I told him to go back to the cottage.

He ignored me and kept butting in on our fun. Tommy told him to go home.

He said, "No." He was becoming a pest.

Tommy noticed some kids swimming on the other end of the lake.

He pointed to them, winked at me, and said in a loud voice, "Hey, Mike, let's shoot those kids over there."

Now we both knew that our BB guns could not shoot that far, but little Bob didn't. Bob looked in the direction Tommy was pointing and saw the kids swimming.

I tried not to laugh as I said, "Yeah, we might hit them in the eye."

We aimed our guns in the direction of the swimmers.

Bob kept looking at the swimmers and back to us, dancing up and down and pleading, "No! No!"

We took steady aim and just as Tommy was squeezing his trigger I saw a little finger slide up over the business end of his BB gun. Bob was going to save the swimmers!

Before I could say anything, Tommy pulled the trigger. The BB gun jumped and the BB hit the tip of Bob's finger.

Time stood still for a second, and then Bob screamed and started to wildly wag his finger while jumping up and down. He immediately took off running and jumping up the path, shaking his finger, and howling like a banshee.

I watched him disappear into the cottage. Everything was quiet for about fifteen seconds.

Suddenly, we heard a roar like a gored bull.

I turned to Tommy and said, "I guess I'll see you tomorrow."

He said "Yeah."

The roaring noise got louder as Dad gathered speed running down the path. Tommy was sent home and I got a whuppin'. My gun was placed in the closet for a couple of hours as I sat inside on the screened-in porch. Even though I technically did not shoot Bob, I was still held accountable. Dad went back to his nap, and when I heard him sawing logs, I was free to slip away.

—⚬—

Although I never shot Bob with my BB gun, I did shoot him with my handmade bow and arrow at home in Flint.

Ken and I had built a small tree house in the vacant lot next to the funeral home, and one day we were playing there.

I had made a bow from a strong, slender branch with lots of spring. I used a piece of leather for the bowstring. For arrows, I selected several long, straight, hollow weed shafts. We fitted big, black thorns into the tips of the arrows and held them in place with wet string that tightened as it dried. Old bird feathers tied to the back of the shaft finished them off. I was quite proud of the workmanship and couldn't wait to try one out.

Suddenly, Bob showed up at the bottom of the tree, even though he was not supposed to wander this far from home. He started to climb up. I told him to go home, but he kept climbing.

Swimming in the lake. Mike swimming by the dock, Ken with facemask, John walking away, and Don facing the camera.

I picked up the bow and slotted an arrow. I leaned over the platform and drew the string back to my cheek, aiming the arrow in his general direction. I told him to go home or I would shoot. He ignored me so I let it fly.

The arrow wobbled in flight and looked like it would miss him, but at the last moment it hit him squarely in the arm and stuck fast.

Bob screamed and jumped down from the tree. The last we saw of him, he was running up Baldwin Street toward home, howling and rubbing his arm.

Ken said, "Looks like you'd better not go home for awhile." Ken had a way of stating the obvious.

—⅏—

All good things eventually come to an end. One day in the early 1960s when I was around twelve years old, Aunt Francis decided to buy the big log cabin on the waterfront at the end of Elk Lake. She was moving into the biggest and best home on the lake and had to sell her little cottage.

Dad put us all in our blue 1960 Chevrolet station wagon with Mom in the front holding a baby. Ken, Bob, and I were in the back seat. We went for one of our famous deer scouting rides in the late afternoon.

Everything was boring and monotonous as usual. Dad drove the

Left to right: John, Don, and Mike. Ken is floating in the water.

dirt roads around the counties of Flint, slowing down and pointing as another deer appeared.

Suddenly everything changed.

Our little ears perked up as Dad said to Mom in a matter-of-fact way that Aunt Francis bought the big log home at the end of the lake and she was selling the cottage.

He went on to say in a more excited way that she was giving him first option to buy the cottage because the kids (us!) loved it so much.

We couldn't believe what we were hearing! We held our breath and leaned forward in the back seat, chins resting on the front seat so we could catch every word.

Dad went on to say that Aunt Francis was going to let him have the cottage, fully furnished, along with the boat, motor, and all of the equipment. The cottage was situated on a lakefront lot with private driveway access. The entire turnkey operation would only cost Dad five thousand dollars.

We had no idea if that was good or bad, and Mom had even less of an idea. Dad spent a lot of time gently explaining to her just how good of a deal this was. The cottage alone was worth three times that amount!

Mom kept whining and saying, "No. It's too much money. We

Playing on the tire swing, Mike is in front with Ken in back.

don't have that kind of money and it will take all of our savings."

Dad became increasingly frustrated when her objections became more whiny and stubborn. This argument seemed to go on for a long time, until Mom played her trump card. She started crying.

Dad didn't buy the cottage. He never forgot it. He should have bought it. He could have flipped it and easily sold it for a tidy profit at fifteen thousand dollars, immediately tripling his savings account. He never forgave Mom for that missed opportunity. And, our up North vacations went down the toilet after that.

We rented a cabin the next year at Wolf Lake and it was not the same. We tried renting a different one the following year. It was not the same either. The vacations quietly slipped away.

—w—

Dad got his real estate license when he retired from the fire department in 1971. He kept looking for that one big deal—the Aunt Francis cottage that he let slip away.

He bought fourteen acres of farmland near Flint and rented it out. The next year, the power company came right through the middle with high voltage lines and they bought a right-of-way. At first, he was really upset until he realized that the money from the right-of-way

Ken drinking water from a pump at a park in West Branch. Bob is pumping and Mike looks on while Mom laughs.

paid for the whole parcel.

He sold the divided land to the farmer and used the profit to buy forty acres in Lapeer County; ten acres of woods and thirty acres of farmland. He rented out the farmland to a local farmer and I spent time hunting in the woods before I went into the Army. It was a nice piece of land, but it was in the middle of nowhere and he eventually sold it to the farmer

When I left home, Dad bought a small lot that was somewhere up North on a lake. It was situated across the street from the lake, not on the water. The second group of kids, John, Don, and Mary, spent several vacations up there.

I visited it once. The lot held a small trailer on a pad, some cheap furnishings, and an fire pit outside. The weekend after he bought it, he moved his things in and put a lock on the trailer.

That same weekend, his trailer was burglarized. Someone called him and he called the sheriff. Dad took Don with him and they met the sheriff at the trailer.

They saw the tire tracks from the truck that supposedly was used to haul away the loot. The tracks went from Dad's trailer straight to the dumpy old cabin at the end of the lake.

Our rental cottage at Wolf Lake. Ken is opening the door, Bob is to his left, John is to his right, and I am checking my BB gun.

Dad fishing off the old bridge in West Branch.

The sheriff said the boys that lived there were crazy.

Dad wanted them arrested, but for whatever reason, the sheriff said he had no proof. The complaint was dropped and the sheriff drove off. Welcome to the lake.

Vacations were never the same again. Dad never did find that Aunt Francis cottage, and I don't think he ever forgave Mom or himself for letting that deal slip away.

CHAPTER SIX

Like so many other kids my age, I attended kindergarten at a public school. It was over a mile from home and, yes, I walked. Mom and Dad drove me the first day of school so they could show me the route. We only had one car and Dad always drove it to work. Mom took me into the school and dropped me off in an open room with other kids my age.

The teacher talked with Mom, who hugged me goodbye and told me to be a good boy.

I remember crying when she left.

At the end of the school day I started my walk home. I had to cross a very busy street with a lady crossing guard.

A man was sitting on his front porch in blue bib overalls drinking a beer, and he told his big, mean-looking dog to "Get 'em!" The dog lunged and hit the fence, snapping and barking!

I cried, and ran as fast as I could.

Another time, the tornado siren was wailing at school and the teacher took us all downstairs into the basement. It got really dark outside and we could hear the wind howling. I cried and the teacher held me and we sang songs.

My walks home were in the afternoon. I liked the sunny days. I did not like the rainy or snowy days. When I got home, Mom had hot soup and a sandwich ready for me. I had a little bookbag for carrying my papers home to Mom and Dad.

One day, I brought home an art project the teacher had us draw. I got an F. She asked us to draw a picture of ourselves. I drew myself as a smiling, stick-boy figure, standing under the bright, shining sun.

The reason I got an F was because I had drawn a big stick between my legs.

The teacher circled the stick and wrote "reflection of the sun" on the top of the paper next to the F, with an arrow pointing to the offending appendage.

My Dad saw this and went ballistic! He was waving the paper, arguing with Mom.

Mom said it was awful.

Dad said, "It looks fine to me!" He put me in the car and we went to school.

He confronted the teacher and they had a "discussion." Dad was yelling at her and she was getting upset.

We finally left and headed home. Dad told me that my drawing was nice, but next time be sure to draw myself with clothes on. This would not be the last time that Dad went to bat for me at school over the years.

—⟶⟶—

▼ Bob carrying his yellow rag dog with his plastic Army pistol.

▲ Bob seated on the bike, Mike on the step behind him, and Ken on the far right.

After kindergarten, I attended St. Agnes School from first grade all the way through high school. Our home was now only four blocks from school and there were a couple of routes I could take, depending on how much time I had.

Our grade school was in the old parish church that had been converted into a school. The classrooms were on the upper floor; the lower floor held the kitchen and big hall that was used for meals, dances, and, of course, Bingo. The parish built a new church and was finishing a new middle and high school building next to our school building.

Nuns and some regular teachers taught us. I fit right in with the discipline and routine. Everything was orderly and clean. If we had to use the bathroom, we raised a hand with either one finger or two fingers extended, showing the teacher which bodily function we needed to perform.

The teachers used big blackboards in the front of the classroom and wrote everything on them with chalk. We had long banners above the chalk boards displaying cursive and block letters. I loved writing the letters and looked forward to writing class.

Of course, the best part of the day was lunch and recess. We ate lunch then went outside to play on the large, blacktopped parking lot. There were no fences to corral us and we just ran wild.

Mike, left, and Ken, right; photos taken by Dad in our backyard circa late 1950s.

Most households had only one car, so almost all of the kids walked to school. We ran, played tag, pushed, shoved, and roughhoused. A nun stood by the building in case anyone needed medical assistance. Usually someone did, for a scraped knee, a bump on the noggin, or broken glasses.

Once I was pushed off the top of a large snow pile where we were playing "King of the Hill" and I hit the back of my head really hard. I had a big goose egg back there and it was tender and hurt.

The nun on the playground said I was fine and sent me back to class. Within about fifteen minutes, the nun teaching my class came by and smacked me on the back of the head with a ruler. I saw stars! Just the encouragement I needed to, "Sit up straight and pay attention."

———

I enjoyed walking to this school. It was much closer and there were no mean men with big, barking dogs. We only had one major intersection to cross at Dupont and Pierson Streets.

At the corner, we were met by a Patrol Boy, an older kid from our school who helped us cross the street. He wore a white Patrol Boy belt that went around his waist and over one shoulder. It folded up into a neat, oval ball and hung on his belt when he was not on duty. It looked like a military uniform belt. All that was needed was a holster and pistol!

The Patrol Boys were big kids we looked up to. When I was older, I volunteered to be a Patrol Boy. It was an official duty that I enjoyed and took very seriously.

———

We were blessed to have a good band program at our school. I started playing the trombone when I was in fifth grade. Our music director, Mr. Joseph Unger, was a very dedicated and talented band director. I went to talk with him about taking lessons. He told me to sit down and he handed me a trombone.

He must have needed trombone players and I looked like a good candidate. He showed me how to hold it, move the slide up and down,

Mike playing the trombone on the front lawn in
his middle school uniform and Patrol Boy belt.

and make some noise by blowing into the mouthpiece.

The slide had seven positions, but I could only reach the first five
because my arms were not long enough. He said that was okay, I
would grow into it. He was right. I liked the trombone.

I took lessons like everyone else in the program and we played as
a band in our practice room in the high school section of the building.
Every year, we played concerts for our parents, and I really enjoyed
being in the band.

The discipline of being part of a team really appealed to me. In
junior high school, I joined the marching band and loved playing at all
the football games. Our little band marched in the half-time shows and
blasted our fight song when the team scored touchdowns.

In high school, our band grew to about 70 members. I was sitting
in fourth chair playing third trombone. First chair was held by the best
trombone player in the school, John Appel. Next to him, Dan Hoodack
played second chair second trombone.

Left to right: Mike with trombone, Bob, John, and Ken standing by our 1960 Chevrolet wagon.

If we wanted to move up a position, we could challenge the person in the chair above us. We played a series of songs and musical tests created and judged by Mr. Unger, who sat in a closet and listened, only knowing us by numbers one or two. The winner moved up and the loser took the lower seat.

I started challenging the two people between John Appel and me. I won the first challenge and moved up to second chair second trombone in ninth grade. Dan Hoodack and John Appel were both juniors, so as a freshman, I decided to sit still for awhile.

Playing second trombone with Dan Hoodack, it didn't take long to realize that I could probably beat him. When I was a sophomore, I decided to challenge him. I won. I was now playing second chair first trombone next to the best trombone player. John Appel taught me a lot about playing my instrument, and he was cool.

In the spring of 1966, our band went to Washington, D.C. to march in the annual Cherry Blossom Festival. We worked hard selling candy bars to raise money and we practiced marching and playing our songs. We couldn't wait to go!

Left to right: Trombonists Ken and Mike in full high school marching band regalia.

The bus trip took about twelve hours, but it was really fun. We stayed in a hotel and we went sightseeing with chaperones. We saw John F. Kennedy's grave with the newly-established eternal flame at its base. It was all very grown up and thrilling.

John Appel graduated when I was a sophomore. I held first chair, first trombone position until I graduated in 1969.

I loved playing in the band. I also played in small jazz and ragtime groups. Every year, I practiced and performed solos and ensembles for competition. My efforts were rewarded with many first place ribbons and the excitement of competition.

In the summer of my junior year, I went to the prestigious Interlochen music camp. The goal of this two-week camp was to bring musicians from the three-state area together to practice and, ultimately, to perform a concert. It was a very intensive camp that demanded a lot of time and hard work.

On the first day, competitions were held to determine one's chair for the remainder of the camp. There were fourteen trombone players at the camp. I was a little self-conscious because my trombone in

St. Agnes High School marching band photo taken in 1965. The band traveled to Washington, D.C. in April, 1966, and marched in the National Cherry Blossom Festival. Mike, third row, standing next to left side tuba with Ken next to him.

its battered case was well-worn and had black electrical tape around a leak near the mouth piece. Several of the other guys had trombones that looked like a million bucks! I decided I would give it my best, and settled down to clean my horn.

We were assigned numbers in a large waiting room. One by one, we were called by number into a smaller room that had a chair, a music stand, and some sheet music on the stand.

The judges were behind a curtain so they could not see us. We were told to sit, look over the music for thirty seconds, and then play it. I concentrated and gave it my best shot.

Later that day, the results were posted on a bulletin board. I held my breath as I moved forward in the crowd, straining to get a look at how I stacked up.

I didn't see my name at once because I looked at the list from the bottom up. I think I gasped as I realized that my name was at the top of the list. I was to hold the position of first chair first trombone!

My excitement quickly turned somber as I realized the enormous pressure this position placed on me to perform and to assist the others. These were the best two weeks of my musical career. I know John Appel would have been proud of me.

—ɷ—

St. Agnes marching band performs on Pennslyvania Avenue in Washington, D.C. Mr. Unger, far right, is in a white director's uniform next to the front row of trombones with John Appel on his right. Ken and I were in the front row blasting out one of the many songs we memorized for the occasion.

Thursday, April 14, 1966 **The Flint J**

WASHINGTON BOUND — Joseph Unger (lower left), St. Agnes Catholic High School band director, goes through a final briefing with his band members before they leave for Washington, D.C. The band left Wednesday for the nation's capital where it will march in the annual Cherry Blossom Festival on Saturday. It was the only Michigan band invited to participate in this year's festival parade. (Journal Photo)

An article about our band trip appeared in *The Flint Journal*. Mr. Unger is in the lower left corner. The white letters mark Ken and me.

When I turned sixteen, all I could think about was getting my driver's license and asked Dad about taking the driver's course.

Dad told me I'd have to wait until next year because he couldn't afford the insurance.

I was deeply upset, but understood. The year dragged by slowly.

Next year, at seventeen, Dad told me I could take the driver's course, get my learner's permit, and eventually my driver's license. I was ecstatic until I heard him say that Ken would be going with me.

Ken had just turned sixteen. I asked Dad how this could be. Since I had to wait a year, shouldn't Ken also wait a year?

He said that the insurance was the same for two as for one, so by this reasoning, Ken could go.

I was really mad and, of course, Ken gloated.

We took a two-week driving course at a school with a professional driving track. The cars we used were new 1967 Chevrolet Chevelles with automatic transmissions.

We had classroom work, tests, and the best part: driving on the track. I did very well, but Ken excelled. We both graduated and earned our learner's permit. We had to drive our family car with Dad until we were ready for the real test.

Dad was a good teacher. He was a professional fire truck driver and he knew all the laws.

I really scared him badly one day. I was making a right turn from a big four-lane highway. I put on my blinker, slowed down and started a snail's turn.

The blast of a truck's air horn behind us and the screaming of air brakes should have given me a clue!

Dad screamed at me, "Step on it! Get around this corner!"

I punched the gas and a big gasoline tanker just missed us as it barreled past us, air horn blaring.

We stopped and I was shaken. Dad was very good. He told me to be more attentive of my surroundings and who is behind me. He also told me not to trust the mirrors alone, but to look over my shoulder. And, to this day, I always look over my shoulder.

—〰—

Ken and I got our driver's license in 1968 and we started driving the battered family station wagon on errands. Dad bought a used 1965 Chevrolet pickup truck and was now driving that to work and to his painting jobs, leaving the station wagon at home for Mom.

The truck had a clutch with a gear shift on the steering column. We wanted to drive the truck, so Dad gave us lessons. I could not get the hang of shifting gears and using that clutch.

Dad got frustrated and quit giving me lessons. Ken took to driving the truck and using the clutch like a pro. I felt like a failure.

Ken took me aside one day and asked if I would let him teach me how to use the clutch.

I thought about it for a second, and agreed.

Ken was the best instructor I ever had. He made me feel comfortable, explained everything, and he didn't yell at me like Dad. I learned very quickly and I was very grateful to him for his help. My brother went on to become a professional truck driver.

—⟋⟍—

Both Ken and I drove the Chevrolet station wagon and Dad's truck to run errands. Try as I might, I never got to drive the car to school. To be completely honest, though, I didn't want to because it was ugly and old. The floor under the driver's seat was rusted out, causing the front seat to fall through the hole. Dad fixed this by jamming a two-by-four under the seat so it caught on the rocker panel and held it up. The seat sat a little higher, but it was no longer falling through the floor.

The floor behind the driver's seat was also rusted out. If we moved the floor mat while Dad was driving, we could look through the hole and see the road race by! We joked about having a Fred Flintstone car.

Ken and I wanted to use the car to go on dates. Washing and cleaning it just didn't make the car look any better. Ken said we should fix the rust holes and paint the old wreck.

The car had two major rust holes above the front headlights that sloshed rain and slush up from the front tires to the windshield while driving. There were also numerous rust holes and spots all over the body, making one wonder if its color was blue or rusty orange.

One day, Dad took the pickup truck to the fire station and wouldn't be home until the next morning. It was time to carry out our plan. We had decided to surprise Dad with his new station wagon.

We jumped into action and found a can of Bondo filler putty in the garage. We read the instructions, mixed the sticky two-part goo, and applied it to the car body, filling in all the holes. For the holes over the headlights, we had to use a section of screen from an old door to stuff in the hole before applying the Bondo.

We spread it on with a wooden paint stir stick and it was very rough. Not to worry as we intended to sand the rough spots smooth.

When we finished applying the sticky goop, we waited about an hour for it to dry. We then started sanding the roughest spots above the headlights first. It made no impact. We rubbed and sanded until our fingers hurt, and nothing changed.

Bondo dries as hard as concrete and you need a sanding machine to make it smooth. We didn't have one, so we left it as it was and moved on to the next step—painting.

We checked Dad's paint inventory in the garage. The only paint we could find was a half gallon of turquoise oil-based house paint. The color looked really nice so we decided to use it.

We gathered a couple of paint brushes, masking tape, drop cloths, and a roller and pan. At first we were very careful, taping the antenna, wipers and chrome parts. We brushed on the paint and used the roller for the large areas like the hood and doors. We skipped painting the roof because no one could see it anyway. We had real trouble trying to trim around the chrome letters "Chevrolet," so we just painted over them.

Mom would peek out the back door every once in a while and say, "That looks nice, boys."

Finally we were all finished. We stepped back to critically admire our work. It looked really good from a distance. We hoped Dad would be pleased.

The next day Dad came home and we were waiting for him in the yard by the car. He got out of the truck and started toward the car. We could tell he was in a good mood.

He said cheerfully, "Hello, boys, whatcha doing?"

We smiled and said, "Nothing!" We tried but failed to suppress our big grins.

Just then he stopped dead in his tracks with a surprised look on his face. He was staring at the car. Several seconds went by with no one moving.

Dad broke the silence and asked, "What did you boys do here?"

He walked over to the car and looked it over. He ran his hand over the rough Bondo above the headlights and made a sound that we could barely hear.

He turned to us, quickly rubbing his hands together, and said, "Good job, boys!"

We told him that we were sorry we couldn't get the Bondo sanded any better. He told us not to worry. The job we did would keep that nasty rain and slush off the windshield.

He thanked us and went inside the house, whistling.

In retrospect, he was awfully happy. His boys had painted his car with turquoise house paint. It really looked terrible from up close.

So why was he so happy?

Mom must have been reporting to him all along by phone as we worked.

About a month later, Dad decided to get another car. He bought a used 1967 gold-colored Chevrolet station wagon. We took the old turquoise station wagon to Sam's Junkyard at the intersection of Pierson and Dort Highways.

Ken and I both loved this old junkyard. Sitting out front was a WWII Autocar U8144T five-ton truck. It was always there to greet you. After the war, the government sold thousands of surplus military trucks to civilians.

These trucks were used by returning servicemen and small businesses for all types of construction and trucking. There was a real shortage of civilian trucks and cars from 1942 to 1945 during the war. All vehicles made during this time were for the military. In 1967, you could still find these trucks tucked away in construction yards and empty lots all over Flint.

Dad drove the old Chevrolet to the junkyard followed by Ken driving Dad's truck. I rode shotgun. We pulled up in front of Sam's little office that was surrounded by junk cars and went in.

Sam was behind the counter chewing on an old cigar and reading the paper.

Dad announced that we had a good car to sell.

Before he could say another word, Sam said without looking up, "Five bucks."

Dad was a little put off and said, "I drove this car here. It's in good shape!"

Sam said, "I don't care if you flew it in. Five bucks." Sam pointed to a big book of preprinted checks, each made out for five dollars, and said, "Take it or leave it."

Dad grumbled and said that he would have to take it. Sam signed a check and handed it to Dad. We left his office and got into our truck.

Dad gunned the truck's engine, put the gear shift in reverse and backed up fast, rammimg the old family Chevrolet in the driver's door.

He yelled, "There ya go! Take that!" and drove off.

I was wondering who really got taken. We didn't talk on the way home. Dad was in a foul mood.

—⟋⟍—

Our high school was attached to our middle and grade schools. When we graduated from eighth grade, it was a simple matter of walking to the end of the hall and through the doors to high school.

We still had nuns teaching our classes, but we also had more lay teachers in the upper grades. Our teachers were dedicated and most of our classes were fun. I enjoyed going to school and hanging out with my friends.

All of this changed, however, the day I became the target of a bully. One of the guys in my freshman class decided to pick on me.

He turned around in class one day when the teacher was out of the room and asked me in a mean voice what I was looking at. He laughed and checked to see if his buddies were watching him. They were. He turned back around and kept asking me what I was looking at and if

I wanted my ass kicked.

I said, "No."

This continued until the teacher walked back into the room.

I was glad she returned because I was feeling sick to my stomach.

The bully was paying attention to the teacher as if nothing had happened. He acted perfectly happy and agreeable.

The teacher gave us a reading assignment and again left the room.

The bully turned around and growled that he was going to beat me up after school. He then said he would let me go. All I had to do was to say, "Please."

I wanted this to end, so I said, "Please."

He laughed and said, "No!"

Everyone laughed and he was on a roll, really having fun at my expense. I realized my mistake and kept quiet, trying hard not to look in his direction.

The bully laughed and jeered, "Say, 'Please,' again!"

I did not. Not because I was brave, but because I was really scared. I could feel everyone staring at us.

Just then the teacher returned to the room and everyone was instantly intent on their reading assignment. I just sat there with my stomach churning.

The bell rang and everyone got up to go to their next class.

The bully got in my face and said he would see me after school to beat me up.

His buddies laughed and they all walked out together, talking about something else.

I don't remember much after that, but I do remember going out a different door when the final bell rang. I had avoided the beating. This routine went on for a week.

The bully taunted me in class to entertain his friends and I avoided eye contact with him. I kept going out a different door each night and was successful in dodging him.

I was having trouble sleeping at night and I didn't want to go to school. I was really glad when the weekend came and I was able to forget about this menace.

Sunday night came too fast. As my family watched *The Ed Sullivan Show* on TV, I was secretly dreading school the next morning. I wanted to tell my dad, but I didn't think he could help me. I was a big guy now.

The next morning, I decided to wait on the corner for Tommy Montpas to come out so I could walk to school with him. He was a year older and was on the football team. I just knew he'd be able to help me.

At last, Tommy came out of his house and headed my way. I made it look like I had just arrived and fell in step with him as we walked along in silence for awhile.

Finally I got up the nerve to tell him about this incident and how sick I was feeling. I asked him if he could help me; if he could talk to the bully.

Tommy said he could help me, but I would have to stand up to this bully all by myself. He explained that I needed to face the bully and that meant that I might have to fight him; that the only way to stop this was through strength. He told me the worst that could happen was that I could get socked in the mouth and roughed up, but that would be much better than how I was feeling.

I was initially disappointed. I expected Tommy to say he would talk to the bully, and if that didn't work he would beat him up. Tommy was not going to do that.

What Tommy did for me instead was so much better. He listened to me. He didn't judge me or belittle me, but he helped me see what I needed to do.

I was skeptical, but I knew that I couldn't continue this way. I thanked him and we talked as we walked on to school. I made up my mind to put an end to the bullying.

It happened in science class. I was sitting in the middle of the window row and the bully was sitting mid front. The teacher gave us some work to do while he stepped out of the classroom.

As if on cue, the bully turned around in his desk to harass me. He was laughing and sneering and his buddies were chuckling.

I said a quick prayer and calmly stood up. My nervous sweat felt like a torrent of ice water running down my sides from my armpits.

I faced the bully, raised my fists, and took a boxer's stance.

In what I hoped was a menacing voice, I said, "Stand up. Let's fight right here, right now."

Time stood still. Everyone turned to look at me.

Some of the girls gasped, others whispered, and they all looked shocked.

What was almost comical was the look of utter surprise on the bully's face. His mouth hung open and he quickly looked around to see if his buddies were there. Before he could reply, the teacher returned.

He looked at me standing up with my fists raised and said, "Morrow, what are you doing? Sit down."

I was happy to comply. The rest of the class went by in a fog. I was thinking about where I was going to meet the bully and how badly he would beat me up.

The bell rang and we all headed out. The bully and his friends left in the first group and disappeared down the hall. I walked out of the classroom and was immediately stopped by Rick Michael. Rick was one of the cool guys and he hung around with the "in" crowd.

He stuck his finger in my chest, looked me in the eye, and said, "Mike, you're okay. If he tries anything, you tell him you're with me."

I thanked him and said I would.

That was the end of it. I was never bothered again. I have never forgotten the help that Tommy and Rick gave me that day. I have used this incident throughout my life to talk with kids about bullying.

I spoke with Rick at our forty-fifth high school reunion. I thanked him for backing me up that day and we had a good talk.

He passed on a couple of years later and I was grateful that I had taken the opportunity to thank him.

—⁂—

I didn't play sports in high school. I tried basketball in ninth grade, but I couldn't dribble. I went out for track in tenth grade and ran hurdles.

I came home one day and told Dad that I came in second in the hurdle race!

He asked me how many kids ran.

I sheepishly replied, "Two."

Band was my talent more than athletics. Jim LaVictoire and I both played in the band. We hung out with Mike Poli and Mike Randall, and enjoyed the perks of watching the football games from the stands as part of the marching band.

Our school's dances were in the large hall on the first floor of the former church. It was exciting to get dressed up and walk to school for these occasions. The lights were soft and a variety of music was played by a local DJ.

The guys hung out in clusters, talking about cars and sports while keeping an eye on the girls on the dance floor. The girls were giggling and whispering, grouped together like antelope around a waterhole.

Jim and I stood on the sidelines, sipping punch. After what seemed like a long time, a slow dance was played.

We both wanted to dance but we didn't have the courage to venture out. We stood there and dared each other to ask a girl to dance. We did a lot of daring and very little asking.

One time, I finally got up my courage to ask a certain young lady to dance. She was in a group of girls in the center of the dance floor. I took a deep breath and started toward her.

Suddenly, it felt like the overhead lights were spotlighting me. All eyes were on me, or so it seemed, as I closed in on the group. On my approach I noticed the girls facing me were watching me closely and whispering to each other.

I just knew they were saying, "Look out, here he comes."

The girl I wanted to ask was facing away from me at a slight angle. I sidled up to the group, took a deep breath, and tapped her lightly on the shoulder. All the girls in the group stopped mid-sentence and just stared. At that moment, I felt like everyone in the entire place was interested in what about to happen. The girl I had just tapped on the shoulder turned to face me.

I said, "Would you like to dance?"

She said, "No," and turned back to the group. They started talking again as if I didn't exist.

I didn't know what to do next. Should I ask someone else in the group or should I turn around and head back to the sidelines?

They say discretion is the better part of valor. I turned around and started back. Despite this public defeat and other awkward attempts at social interaction, I had fun at the dances and I did get to dance with lots of girls.

Jim and I discussed the evening as we walked home and talked about how we could improve our chances for the next dance.

The dances were great, but we also had to attend school. My favorite class in high school was drafting. I really liked the precision and skill it required to produce a drawing of an object for manufacture.

From an early age, I had the ability to draw, instinctively understanding the principles of perspective and vanishing point. I doodled and drew pictures at home and in school, creating drawings of airplanes, cars, rocket ships, and people.

My talent for art helped me immensely with my drafting classes. Drafting, in turn, helped to improve my artwork. I have kept many of my drawings from grade school through high school in a large binder.

I was one of the artists for the high school newspaper. During my

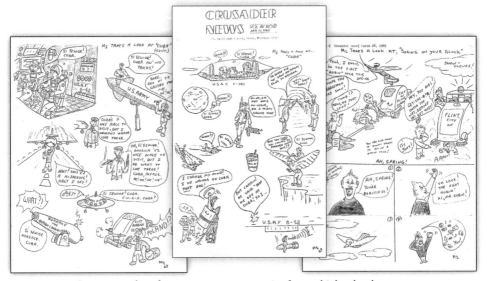

Some examples of my cartoon commentaries for my high school paper.

junior and senior years, my cartoons tackled the issues of the day, often targeting the people and events that made the news headlines both at school and nationwide.

I created a special full-page section of cartoons highlighting the airplane highjacking craze that swept the country in 1968 and 1969.

As Yearbook Art Editor, I designed and drew the cover and my cartoons were scattered throughout its pages. I had a blast working at this extracurricular activity. I loved the interaction with other staff members and, dare I say, the fame that it brought.

We were fortunate that Jim LaVictoire saved every edition of the school newspaper from ninth through twelfth grade. Fifty years later, I scanned his entire archive in order to share them electronically with our classmates via DropBox.

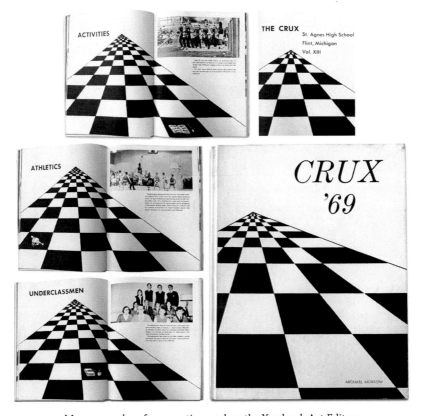

More examples of my creative work as the Yearbook Art Editor.

When I graduated from high school in 1969, I bought my first car with the cash I'd saved up. It was a 1962 Chevrolet Impala SS and cost five hundred dollars.

This, however, was not my first choice. The first car I looked at was a 1966 Pontiac GTO. It had a huge engine with a Hurst four-speed shifter on the floor. It was sitting at a used car lot on Pierson and Clio Roads and the sign on the windshield read twelve hundred dollars.

The salesman saw I was enthralled with it and he said, "Take her for a spin, kid."

I settled in and started her up. The engine rumbled as the tachometer quivered. I shifted into first gear and carefully drove her off the lot.

I gripped the wood-trimmed steering wheel and roared off down Clio Road. I quickly shifted from first to second; then, gaining speed, the tach jumped as I shifted to third gear. The engine screamed, and I slammed it into fourth gear. I was flying!

I knew I had to have it. I took her back to the salesman and told him I would be back with the money.

I walked home and told Dad that this was just the car I needed!

He looked at the price, did some math on the insurance, and said, "You can't afford it."

I was really upset; I loved that GTO!

Dad said he would help me look for a car.

Instead of the GTO, I ended up with the Impala SS; it was still a muscle car, but one I could afford. When I floored the gas pedal, I watched the speedometer going one way and the gas gauge going the other way! But it was okay. Gas was only twenty-seven cents a gallon.

CHAPTER SEVEN

My first jobs for hire were cutting lawns,
raking leaves and shoveling snow. I liked these kinds of jobs because I
was my own boss, and with hard work, I made a lot of money.

It all started at the worn, green Formica kitchen table. Dad sat there
working on bills with a bottle of beer, and his pen and paper. There
were no computers, calculators, or cell phones back then to help balance our family's budget. He figured out which bills would be paid in
cash and which ones called for a money order. He did a lot of head-
scratching in between.

He called me over to the table and said it was time to talk about my
allowance. This was great news since I wasn't getting an allowance! In
my head, I was trying to calculate how much money I'd need and if
Dad would give me that much.

Dad burst my bubble when he started the lecture by saying I was
not going to get an allowance. He said that he and Mom provided us
with room, board, clothes, and school supplies.

He handed me a little spiral notebook and a blue Bic pen and said
I would need these to write down the names and addresses of my
customers.

Customers? What was he saying?

Dad went on to say that if I wanted money I had to earn it. He took
me outside and pointed to the old family push mower and said that it
was now mine. He also handed me a pair of grass clippers and a rake.

He explained how to go about getting customers by knocking
on doors and asking the home owners if I could cut their grass. He

explained about doing a quality job and building a reputation for honesty and good work.

Dad even told me how much I should charge. A small lawn, front and back, should be fifty cents, and a large corner lot could go for seventy-five cents. He said I could work after school and on weekends but my homework had to be finished.

He ended the lesson by saying that I would do our lawn and the widow woman's lawn next door for free before I went out to make money.

Since Ken and I did a lot of things together, I quickly enlisted his help in this project and we set out to get customers.

We started our Saturdays by cutting our small lawn and the neighbor's lawn and then we looked for paying customers. The neighbor on the other side of our house, Mr. Whitaker, was Dad's drinking buddy and he was fair game.

We knocked on his door and asked if we could cut his grass.

To our surprise he said yes. He didn't even balk when we said it would cost fifty cents!

We did a good job, and when we went to be paid, Mr. Whitaker gave us a dollar and said to come back again next week. We had our first customer and he overpaid us! It was starting out to be a good day.

We immediately went to the next neighbor, Mr. McGonagall, who lived behind us and asked him if we could cut his grass.

He said yes, but he wanted us to use his Lawnboy power mower.

This was almost too good to be true. His yard was a double lot, so using the power mower made the job go very quickly. When we finished, we again received a dollar and were told to come back next week.

Ken said we were asking too little for our work since both of these customers gave us a dollar.

I reminded him that they were Dad's friends, so let's see how we do when we get further from home.

As it turned out, the pricing strategy Dad laid out was just about right. Most people were happy to pay fifty cents and their yards were not that big. We found out that if we asked for a dollar, more often than not, people would decline and close the door. We settled down to a pretty lucrative business, cutting lawns on Saturdays during the summer and into the fall.

Our parents made us save half of what we earned and my mother opened individual savings accounts for Ken and me.

Ken loves to tell the story of how Mom opened his savings account.

She used his 1894 silver dollar that Grandpa had given each of us kids. He tells how the clerk probably grabbed her wallet and swapped out his silver dollar for her paper dollar.

Ken never forgave Mom for doing that. I don't know how, but I managed to hang on to my silver dollar and I still have it today.

The lawn mowing turned into snow shoveling in the winter and we continued to shovel in the money. Our bank accounts grew and we had extra money to buy models, candy, and go to the movies.

Ken grew tired of the work and we had a falling out over our pricing one day. There was a large corner lot two blocks from home that we were cutting for a dollar using the lady's power mower. Ken wanted to charge more and cut out all of the smaller jobs. I, of course, liked the way we did it, so we parted company.

Ken went back to the lady on the corner and got the job for two dollars, but that was the only lawn he did. I kept up with the remaining yards we had, but didn't have a lot of time for other things.

It's interesting to look back and wonder why we never decided to buy a power mower to grow our business. I guess the answer is that we were too young and life got in the way. As we grew older, our time was consumed with band practice, school events, and other things— like girls.

—⚊—

As a fireman, Dad worked one 24-hour shift and then had two days off. On his off days, like all the firemen, he did other jobs to supplement his income. Dad's older brother, Delaus, was also a fireman. He and Dad tried their hand at concrete work.

I used a sledge hammer to help my Dad break up Mrs. McGilvery's old concrete driveway next door. Then I helped him hand mix and pour her new driveway. It was hard work, but my father seemed to thrive on hard work.

When I was much younger, Dad had decided to replace our old gravel driveway with concrete. Wanting to save some money, he did the work himself. Since we were too little to help, we just stayed out of the way and watched.

Dad had someone come in with a tractor and grade out the existing gravel and dirt. Next, a big dump truck delivered a load of sand. The truck backed into our driveway and started to dump the load. Suddenly, Dad yelled to stop, but it was too late. As the dump bed was rising, it caught the telephone line and broke it. After some cursing and some head-scratching, the driver fixed the line.

Dad had rented a small electric cement mixer that had a rotating barrel and rolled around on wheels. He mixed a batch of concrete by shoveling in precise amounts of sand, gravel, and cement. The mixer tumbled the batch as he sprayed water in the revolving opening to wet the mix and turn it into a slurry.

Once the slurry was mixed to his satisfaction, he dumped the concrete into the wooden forms and created the next little section of the driveway. He did this many times until he had a ten-foot by ten-foot section completed. He then floated a board across the forms, smoothing the concrete into a perfect, flat surface. He topped it off by trimming the edges with a troweling tool. It was hard, hot, work in the summer sun.

Having just finished dumping a load, Dad was getting ready to reposition the rotating mixer. Mom was on the little back porch holding a baby and Ken and I were in the work area watching Dad.

Dad reached down and took hold of the mixer; he started to shake violently. His whole body began convulsing, jerking up and down, while he made guttural moaning sounds. Dad was being electrocuted by a faulty ground wire in the mixer!

As he jerked up and down, and Mom laughed at the peculiar sight and exclaimed, "Look, boys, Daddy's dancing!" Completely unaware of the mortal danger he was in, she clapped her hands and sang,

"Dance, Daddy, dance!"

We didn't think Dad was dancing, but he sure was doing something!

Suddenly, Dad broke free. He arched his back, screamed in agony, and yanked his hands away from the mixer. He stood weakly, shaking his hands, and dripping with sweat. Mom stopped singing.

When he regained his strength and his bearings, Dad yelled at her. Just like a trapdoor spider, she vanished inside.

Dad and Delaus worked hard to make their little concrete business a success. Delaus owned an old 1951 Ford pickup truck that they used for the work.

Since they both had families, there was not a lot of money to buy equipment. The small jobs they got didn't make enough money to compensate for all the time, effort, and rental equipment they needed to make the business profitable.

I heard them talking in the kitchen one time about how they screwed up a job and the customer was not too happy. They had been hired to pour a garage floor with a center drain. When they finished, they were surprised when the water ran away from the drain and not toward it! Seems it was a big deal to the owner. That job probably led to each one going his own way in search of different part-time work.

—◊◊◊—

My father found his niche as a house painter and he was very good at it. Guess who his number one helper was? That's right, me! He started my painting career when I was about ten years old.

He brought home a carload of screens and storm windows and I lined them up in the garage, scraped them, and painted them. We always did two coats of paint. I had to be careful painting screens as the mistakes always stood out.

Dad would come home, inspect them, and either say, "Good job," or correct my mistakes. Ken also helped. These small jobs were not too bad and they didn't eat up a lot of our free time.

One day, Dad decided that we were big enough to go with him on a job. Ken was always taller than me by about an inch; and, if we didn't slouch, we looked like big kids.

So he took us both to help out on one of his big jobs. He was hired to paint a very large two-and-a-half story wood-sided home for a doctor. It had tons of wooden storm windows and screens that all had to be taken down, cleaned, and painted. The house was only in fair shape, which meant that we had to wash and scrape all of the flaking paint by hand.

My dad did the high ladder work and Ken and I concentrated on the lower levels. It was already very hot and muggy and only 9:00 a.m.!

Mom had packed our lunch in a paper bag and we brought the big green Thermos jug filled with ice water. When Dad decided it was lunch time, we cleaned ourselves up a little with rags and sat under a big oak tree in the back yard.

Dad handed each of us a bean sandwich wrapped in wax paper. Yes, you heard it right—a pork and bean sandwich with Miracle Whip. You can imagine how sloppy those were. We were hungry so we ate them and they weren't too bad.

I asked Dad why we couldn't go to McDonald's for lunch.

"Because it costs money," he said.

We washed down the soggy bean sandwiches with ice water, and for desert Mom had packed Hostess cupcakes! To this day, I still have a pork and bean sandwich with Miracle Whip from time to time and remember the fun times of eating lunch under a tree in some stranger's backyard.

After lunch we started scraping and priming all the bare wood spots we could find on the house. We used white oil-based paint to prime these areas and we got more on us than on the wood.

It was hot, sticky work and there was never a breeze. After we primed the house, we painted the first coat. This was the most important coat because it had to cover everything.

After the first coat, we did the second coat. If you missed a small spot on this coat, it wouldn't show, so this second coat seemed to go faster. Last, we rehung all the screens and put the storm windows in the garage.

We worked on this house for almost two weeks and my dad was paid seven hundred fifty dollars. I thought we were rich, until I saw

Dad working on the bills at the kitchen table and making little piles of money to pay them.

When Dad went to the grocery store in the 1960 Chevrolet station wagon, he put all the back seats down and packed the car with brown paper grocery bags full of food. Upon his return, we all formed a relay line and passed the groceries from the car into the house. The line seemed to take forever because that's what it took to feed a family of eight!

Halfway through the grocery bag relay, he waved a very long register tape and yelled to Mom, "Ma, the price of everything is going up! I paid nearly sixty dollars for this load!"

—⚬⚬—

Dad continued house painting through the 1970s and then slowed down after that. It was a one-man show; he never expanded.

One time while helping him on a job, I asked why he didn't get a truck and hire a couple of workers to do several jobs at the same time.

He never really had a good answer; and I realized later, as an adult, that either he never wanted to expand or he was afraid of failure.

His disinterest in pushing the boundaries stayed with him his entire life. He was not lazy; he worked very hard but was content with his lot in life.

—⚬⚬—

In 1970, I bought a 1962 three-quarter ton Chevrolet pickup truck for two hundred fifty dollars. The body was all patched and primed with gray paint. It had a 4-speed stick shift on the floor and wooden racks for hauling junk.

The guy selling it said he had just overhauled the engine. I knew zip about engines. He showed me it was spotless and clean, had new parts, and it ran well.

I bought it for cash and drove it home. My plan was to clean out people's basements, sell the good stuff to antique stores, and take the rest to the junk yard. In those days, you could dump a load at the junkyard on Dort Highway for five bucks.

I parked the truck in front of our house. Before I could realize my dream of becoming a junkman extraordinaire, the engine blew. My friend, Dallas, who worked on his 1968 Baracuda came over and looked at my truck.

He said that the engine had indeed been overhauled, but it looked like the guy had not replaced the cam shaft.

I asked if that were a big job.

Dallas said we would have to tear the engine down, replace the cam shaft, get new seals, and then put her back together.

I asked about the cost and he said around one hundred dollars and he and I would do all the work. I was very interested. I could get my truck fixed and learn something in the process.

I asked Dad what he thought.

He said there was no guarantee that we could fix it and I would be throwing good money after bad. He told me to sell the hunk of junk and take my loss.

Something told me I should let Dallas try to fix it. However, I listened to my dad and sold the truck for seventy-five dollars to a man who owned a towing company.

About two months later, I was driving by the man's business when I saw my truck sitting outside his shop. It was painted bright yellow with his logo emblazoned on the door and had a towing boom in the bed.

I stopped and went in to see him. I told him the truck looked beautiful and asked what had been the problem with the engine.

He said the overhaul was fine; all it needed was a cam shaft.

I left feeling happy for him but sad for myself for not listening to my gut that told me to fix my truck.

I also didn't follow my idea to collect junk. Who knows—it could have been the start of the 1-800-Got-Junk company! I learned a pivotal lesson that day. Always trust my instincts.

—⁓—

Dad paid Ken and me for our painting work, but he couldn't afford to pay us much. We usually got a five dollar bill for a week's work. I was not always happy with that arrangement, and the older I got, the more money I hoped to be paid.

Dad answered by saying that he provided my room and board, clothes, school fees, etc. So when I turned sixteen, I started looking for a better job.

My search for employment began one Saturday. Not having a car at this point, I walked or rode my bike everywhere I went.

I applied at Uncle Louie's, a local Coney Island grease pit, and was hired on the spot for a dollar an hour.

I went home and told Dad about my new job.

He said he didn't want me working around those hot grease cookers, so I went back and told them I didn't want the job. Dad was right about a sixteen-year-old kid and hot grease. It was an accident waiting to happen.

I then came across a local soft-serve ice cream store that was just opening. I sat at a table with three other kids my age while some guy explained to us what we would be doing for a dollar an hour.

He finished, turned to me, and said, "But we are going to pay you a dollar and ten cents an hour because you will be the evening assistant manager!"

My head immediately began to swell and I sat a little taller in the booth and listened closely to his next words.

He said I would be responsible for cleaning up and closing the store, as well as taking the cash deposit to the bank's night drop box, among other tasks.

His voice droned on but I had already tuned him out. This was not the job for me for a lousy ten cents more per hour.

I continued walking down the road and came to the strip mall at Pierson and Clio Roads. This was about four miles from our home, on the very western edge of the city.

I went into the big Cunningham Drugstore that was at the center of the strip mall. Cunningham's had a pharmacy and drug counter in the rear of the store but they also sold everyday items, just like today's Walgreens, plus they sold alcohol.

The crown jewel of the store was the lunch counter. It had those round, red cushioned stools, and little jukeboxes on the countertop. There was a big grill where a pretty girl in a white uniform made cheeseburgers. This place looked great!

I told the lady at the cash register that I was looking for a job and she sent me to the back of the store to see Mr. Bennett, the owner. He was sitting at his desk smoking his pipe and doing paperwork.

I told him I was looking for a job and we talked. He did most of the talking.

I nodded my head with an appropriate, "Yes, sir," every so often.

Before I knew it, I was hired as a stock boy and, to my delight, I was going to make one dollar thirty-five cents an hour!

Mr. Bennett told me when to report for work and that Rick, the senior stock boy, would teach me the ropes.

Rick was three years older and I looked up to him as having all the answers. He taught me how to sweep the floor using a large push broom and sweeping compound that looked like brown, sticky saw-dust. It caught all the dust bunnies and debris on the floor; it also marked where I had swept. I was amazed and couldn't wait to tell Mom about this new idea for sweeping floors.

He showed me how to unload trucks, stock shelves, and break down the cardboard boxes for storage above the rest rooms. Every week, we threw them away in a big dumpster as there was no recy-cling back in those days.

There was a big furnace in the back area of the store. It had a large concrete door that opened by pulling on a steel cable that lowered a counterweight and slid the door up.

We burned just about everything that would burn and some stuff that wouldn't. Rick taught me to be careful around the furnace and I paid close attention. However, the other new hire, Bob, did not.

Like me, Bob was a stock boy in training with Rick. We ended up on a shift overlap one Saturday and we were cleaning out a closet and burning trash.

Bob was filling a wastebasket with stuff and I was burning it. I opened the heavy concrete door and dumped the loaded basket into the roaring fire.

I was standing in front of the open furnace door poking the fire with a metal rod when Bob called me. I pulled the heavy door closed, turned away, and started walking over to the closet.

At that instant, there was a very loud Boom! followed by a jarring Clang! as the huge concrete door was blown off its track by a massive explosion in the furnace.

The room was immediately filled with thick, black, smoke.

The door to the back area flew open. Mr. Bennett, outlined in the white light from the front of the store and surrounded by smoke, yelled, "What in the hell is going on in here?

I told him the furnace blew up, and we opened all the doors and windows to clear out the smoke.

When I asked Bob what he had thrown in the basket, he said he was throwing out all of the old aerosol spray paint cans.

I explained to him that those were highly flammable and that we could have been killed! It took us quite a while to clean up that mess.

—⁓—

Taking my breaks at the soda fountain was one of my favorite things. Each week, Cunningham's gave its employees a coupon book with little red tickets worth ten cents each and totaling several dollars. Each payday, I was given a coupon book of tickets based on how many hours I had worked the week before.

Sometimes, I used my coupons to buy a soda for twenty-five cents, or, if on a lunch break, a cheeseburger. A girl named Donna worked behind the counter and she was a knockout. I loved to order from her and watch her make a cheeseburger.

She was probably either nineteen or twenty when I was seventeen. Her hair was blonde and her skirts were short. She drove a black 1965 Chevrolet Impala SS and wore a black leather jacket. She smacked her chewing gum constantly and hung out with guys like the characters from *Grease* or *Happy Days*. Donna was always nice to me and she gave me extra fries with my burger.

One day I was hanging around the main cash register and the cashier asked if I would like to learn how to run the register.

I said, "Sure," jumping at the chance to learn something new.

She was very patient with me as she went through how to ring up purchases, use the register, and count money. It was a slow time of day and a man brought his purchase to the register.

She explained that she was training me and asked if he would mind having me ring him up.

He said, "No, that will be fine." I took his single purchase and punched the keys for two dollars and thirty-five cents.

The keys were individual buttons with numbers on them that I had to punch separately to make up the correct price. I looked at the tax chart that was taped on the register, added the appropriate tax, and hit the total.

The cash drawer opened and the man gave me a twenty dollar bill. I started to put the bill in the drawer with all the other store money when the cashier stopped me.

She explained that I should always lay the money on the cash register drawer sill so everyone can see it. Then I should count out the change and then count the change back to the customer, placing it in his hand. That way, there was no confusion or dispute over the denomination of the bill the customer gave you. I did this and, when the customer was satisfied with the transaction, placed the twenty dollar bill in the drawer.

The man thanked me and the cashier thanked him for his patience. We were taught to always be polite to customers and to each other.

Under her watchful eye, I worked the cash register for about half an hour and then went back to my stock boy duties. Learning this skill of serving a customer and counting back money correctly, instead of giving the customer a handful of change wrapped in a wrinkled receipt, served me well throughout my entire life.

—⋘—

At Cunningham's, many life lessons and skills were learned, and I really enjoyed working there. Not long ago, I looked back on my Social Security records to find that they started in 1967 with Cunningham's Drugstore. I made five hundred and forty-four dollars that year—a lot of money for a young sixteen-year-old kid.

When I was seventeen, most of my time was consumed by my schoolwork and extra-curricular activities, like band. My hours at Cunningham's shrank as school started in earnest.

I had to walk or bike about four miles one way to get to work. Going home in the evening, it was always dark. Finally, I couldn't juggle both without a car or a ride so I reluctantly quit my job.

My senior year, I went to work at Federal Department Store, which was closer than Cunningham's. Federal was one block from my school, in a little strip mall with several other stores. I was hired to work in the sporting goods department as salesman, stock boy, and all around do-whatever-needed-to-be-done kind of guy.

I enjoyed working at Federal, especially in the sporting goods section, and made almost two dollars an hour. I ate my meals or snacks in the break room. With only vending machines available, the break room was a far cry from Cunningham's lunch counter.

My training at Cunningham's paid off, having taught me how to ring up purchases, properly count change, and talk to customers. I kept my small sporting goods area neat and clean.

Sporting Goods was on the lower level to the right of the escalator. It consisted of four rows of double-sided shelves and an L-shaped counter against the wall. The guns sat in racks behind the counter where high-dollar items were locked inside, displayed behind glass.

I bought my first .22 caliber rifle from that store. It was a Marlin Golden Mountie lever action carbine. I loved shooting that rifle and felt like a real cowboy carrying it in the woods.

I also purchased a .177 caliber Crossman M1 carbine BB rifle with a wooden stock. It was an exact replica of the real rifle and was fun to shoot. In order to cock the gun, I had to grip the barrel and pull it back until the spring engaged. I was careless one day and my index finger was over the barrel as I cocked it. The gun misfired and the BB went into my finger, severing my tendon and lodging on the back side of my finger bone. Dad took me to a local doctor who removed the BB and sewed my tendon back together in his office. Chalk up another gun safety lesson learned the hard way.

CHAPTER EIGHT

I graduated from high school in early May of 1969. Having left Federal, I thought about looking for another job. However, my real goal was to join the Army.

I talked with my dad and he said I needed to go to college to get the diploma to hang on the wall—something he never got. When he returned home from WWII, Dad had hoped to attend college on the GI Bill, but his widowed mother needed his income to help support the family.

I wanted to go to an art school near Detroit.

Dad said no and, instead, encouraged me to leverage my natural

Jim, left, and Mike with Mike's 1962 Impala SS after graduation.

talent for art by studying engineering. I had enjoyed drawing for my school's newspaper and yearbook and had hoped those skills might be marketable. So I enrolled in a two-year course of study leading to an associate's degree in Mechanical Design Technology from Mott Community College.

Even though I had money saved from my lawn cutting and snow shoveling business, it was a shock to see how much college was going to cost. My parents could not afford to pay for my school, so I would be responsible for tuition and books. I decided to look for a real summer job.

I needed employment that would work around my college schedule and had always liked the idea of working for the railroad. Jim and I used to talk about jumping in an empty boxcar and riding the rails.

I fantasized about switching boxcars in the freight yard and riding on trains, thinking that would be a really cool job. I never did any research and had no idea where the railroad hiring office was located. It was getting late in the afternoon, so I decided to look for it in the morning.

On the way home from my job search, I stopped at the Fisher Body assembly plant and filled out a job application just for practice. Because those jobs paid really well—more than five dollars an hour— I had little hope of being hired. Everyone wanted to work there.

I got a phone call before supper that same afternoon from the factory. A woman told me my application was approved and I was to start work the next morning at 8:00 a.m.

While I should have been ecstatic over being hired, I was actually a little bummed to be starting work the same week as my graduation. No goof off time with my friends and, worse still, it looked like my aspirations of railroad work were rapidly fading.

I reported the next morning and the first thing I noticed was how large the parking lot was. It sprawled over many acres and was filled with cars.

The parking lot led me to a two-story box building. It was made up of row upon row of dirty green windows running the entire length of both floors. Entering through the visitor's door, I was thrilled to actually be inside this huge, sprawling, assembly line plant. The noise was deafening and the building was alive with activity.

I was escorted to the employment office. As we walked through part of the plant, my senses were overwhelmed by an industrial calliope of loud, sharp noises, acrid smells, sparks from welding machines, and a myriad of men and machines in constant motion. I was worried about getting lost in this vast factory and having to ask for directions back to the parking lot.

In the office, I filled out some paperwork and sat through a fifteen-minute film on safety with about ten men also starting that day. Once we were finished, someone walked me to my new workstation and turned me over to my foreman, Art.

Art showed me my locker and gave me a quick run down on breaks and lunch. I got two five-minute breaks, one before and one after my half-hour lunch break. He introduced me to Tommy, another eighteen-year-old, who was a polite young man from Tennessee. Tommy would be working opposite me on the assembly line.

Our plant made Buick bodies. The frames started out in the basement and rode on large individual car dollies with small metal wheels. Robots welded the car frames while a heavy metal chain running in a semi-enclosed slot in the floor pulled the dollies along.

When the cars were ready to go up to the next level, the chain looped down into the floor and the dollies were snagged by another chain that pulled the car bodies up a steep incline to the next level.

Tommy and I were stationed at the end of the first floor where the chain line hauled the cars up to the floor above. Art was very big on safety and told us never to stand on the chain or to cross it while it was moving. Watching those hundreds of heavy car bodies being pulled along by that powerful chain impressed me to do exactly as Art said—stay away from that chain!

Art then showed me my job. Tommy and I performed identical tasks on opposite sides of the car body.

First, as the car body approached, I took a rounded chisel and heavy hammer and pounded the upper and lower corners of the empty windshield frame. Art explained that the windshields often did not fit properly and this little bit of extra pounding made it possible to slide them right in. Made sense to me.

Next, I picked up a slab of black putty and followed Art to the rear of the car. He showed me the areas to plug up with the putty so carbon monoxide would not leak into the car. Apparently, those robotic welders did not always do such a good job and there were plenty of holes.

Each body style was different and the worst of the lot were the station wagons. They seemed to require a lot of attention and about a quarter of a brick of putty.

After Art left, a siren sounded throughout the factory and rotating lights flashed, warning of assembly line startup. The line jerked to life with a loud clanging heard and bumping felt throughout the shop. With all the clanking and jolting of car bodies, it sounded like a freight train waking up in the yard.

It didn't take long for me to realize that I was trapped like a fly on flypaper to this spot. The car bodies rolled by at a fair clip and I was worried about not getting all my tasks done. Tommy was a big help. He'd been working this spot for a while and he would point out things to me as needed.

Our first five-minute break started when the line ground to a halt. Tommy, being an old hand, sprinted for the bathroom and I followed.

Fortunately, our workstation was right near the rest rooms so we made it with time to spare. I watched as the old timers smoked and joked. Before I knew it, the siren sounded and we were back on the line.

The highlight of my work day, just like at school, turned out to be lunch. This sounds like something a kid says when his parents ask, "What was your favorite thing at school today?"

At noon, the line stopped for thirty minutes. I soon learned to dash to the rest room, take care of business, and grab my old gray battered lunch box. I then hustled back to the last steel-framed car body I had just finished, climbed inside, and wolfed down my lunch—including a Hostess cupcake or Twinkie. Then I could relax for a few minutes. If I fell asleep, the sirens and the lurching of the car body would wake me up and I would simply jump out and start all over again.

Assembly line work was boring. We did the same set of tasks on the passing car bodies from the time the line started until the siren blew and the line stopped. I sometimes wondered what kept people doing this kind of work. But every Friday when I received my paycheck, I knew the answer.

I made more money than I knew what to do with. At eighteen years old, I was making almost six dollars an hour—totaling two hundred thirty dollars a week, and usually more with overtime.

Despite being flush with cash, I hated the overtime and just wanted to go home at the end of my shift! However, my earnings tipped nearly eighteen hundred dollars in 1969, because of overtime, and paid for college, my car, and my living expenses.

We had to work overtime almost every Friday and most days in between. We got the word as it was passed down the line. Everyone would simply yell to the next guy the number of overtime hours we were required to work.

The man who did the grinding on the cars one floor above ours was a deaf mute. Since he couldn't speak, he'd bang on a piece of metal with a pipe to get our attention. Then his fingers flashed the number of overtime hours.

One Friday evening, he was so excited he actually hooted while flashing three fingers for three hours of overtime! I had a date that night and I just wanted to leave—but I made money instead.

Tommy and his wife had moved from Tennessee for better job opportunities. They were fortunate as Tommy's wife worked in the factory office. They both loved their jobs and the money.

Tommy and I spent a lot of time talking and we learned a lot about each other. Tommy said his goal in life was to work on the assembly line just long enough to become a plant truck driver. These men drove the big auto carriers that moved car bodies from the north plant to the south plant—a distance of about one mile. I didn't really know what I wanted after college, but I knew it wasn't assembly line work or anything to do with a factory.

—◊—

One day Tommy and I were doing our same old routines and waiting for lunchtime.

Suddenly I heard Tommy scream, "Mike, help me! Help me!"

I looked up and saw Tommy standing on the moving assembly line chain and his foot was caught in it. He was standing behind a station wagon that was beginning its climb to the next floor. The chain was looping down into the floor and Tommy's foot was about to go with it.

Art had warned us over and over, "Don't stand on the line!" But Tommy had gotten careless. The emergency shut off button that would immediately stop the line was about twenty feet away.

I made a snap decision that ended up saving Tommy's foot and, quite possibly, his life. I lunged at Tommy and tackled him, pushing him off the line. His foot came out of his boot and the boot was crushed as the chain disappeared into the slot in the floor. Tommy was rattled and bootless, but otherwise okay.

Art came by and saw Tommy standing with only one boot and knew immediately what had happened.

He chewed us both out and told us how lucky we were, and then he gave Tommy another boot. We went back to work, thoroughly shaken, but glad to be in one piece.

—\\\\—

In the early spring of 1970, my parents sold our family home on Baltimore Boulevard and moved to 434 Oakwood Street in Flushing. Dad wanted to move out of the city. They found a nice ranch home in a quiet little subdivision about thirty miles from our old address.

One weekend, Ken and I loaded our belongings and the family furniture into Dad's 1965 Chevy pickup and made many trips to our new home.

I lived there for about a month. My dad loved to give orders when he was drinking. One Saturday morning, he told all of us boys to load up in the car; it was time to go to the barber college for haircuts.

Dad had taken us there ever since we were old enough to get our hair cut. He loved it. If we went to the beginning barbers, we could get a haircut for a quarter!

One time, when Ken and I were about seven or eight years old, our routine summer buzz cuts were anything but routine. Ken must have wiggled (although he says he didn't) and his barber cut his ear really good.

Dad came in just as they stopped the bleeding. They told him not to worry; Ken's haircut was free!

When we drove home, Dad looked at Ken with the big bandage on his ear and said, "Good job, Kenneth. Next time, wiggle some more!"

Looking back now, it all seems funny and I get his sense of humor. We didn't get it then.

Since I was eighteen, a high school graduate, and a factory worker, I asked Dad if I could get my own haircut.

He said, "No. If you are living in my house, then you have to live by my rules or get the blankety-blank out!"

I said, "Okay," and headed for the basement where Ken and I shared a room and started packing my meager belongings in cardboard boxes.

My brother looked at me and asked me what I was doing.

I told him that I did not want to live by Dad's rules so I was getting the blankety-blank out!

"You can't do that," he said.

"Watch me."

I went upstairs with my first box and put it in my car. Dad was sitting at the kitchen table drinking a beer.

When I came up with my last box and some clothes, Dad finally noticed me.

He asked me what I thought I was doing.

"You said that I have to live by your rules in your house or get out. I don't agree with your rules, so I'm getting out."

He glared at me and yelled, "You can't do that!"

"Watch me."

I loaded the last box, backed out of the driveway and started driving. I didn't know where I was going; I just headed for downtown Flint.

I ended up on First Street early that Saturday afternoon. After scanning the local newspaper for apartment rental ads, I found myself standing in front of an old two-story brick house. A man holding the same newspaper walked up next to me. We spoke and he introduced himself as Bill. He was about thirty, married, and lived in Ohio. He was an engineer with General Motors and had just received a promotion to work in the Flint office for a year.

I introduced myself and explained that I was an engineering student at Mott Community College and was working on the assembly line at Fisher Body.

Bill asked if I were planning to rent an apartment.

I said, "Yes. I was hoping to look at this one."

"How about sharing this apartment and splitting the rent?" he asked. "I'll be here Monday through Friday morning and in Ohio Friday evening through Monday morning."

I didn't know this man from Adam, but he seemed like a very genuine person. The arrangement sounded good, so I agreed.

We went to the door and the landlady showed us a two-bedroom apartment upstairs. It had a single bathroom papered in green wallpaper with frogs on it. Upon closer inspection, someone had drawn mustaches on all of the frogs.

On the other end of the apartment, there was a tiny kitchenette. The large living room-dining room featured a big round oak table and chairs. Two windows faced the street and we could actually climb out and sit in an old chair on the flat roof of the porch.

The house was in decent repair and the apartment was sparsely furnished. Rent was thirty dollars a week or one hundred twenty dollars a month, payable on the first. This was great! Splitting the rent, my share was just sixty dollars a month.

This living arrangement worked out extremely well. Bill and I both worked in the daytime, and in the evenings he helped me with some of my harder college subjects like math and hydraulics. True to his word, Bill visited his family in Ohio every weekend and I had the place all to myself.

—〜〜—

I really enjoyed the freedom that living in that apartment gave me; however, going to college and working didn't leave me much free time. Jim started nagging me about going to Florida for spring break. And, admittedly, it sure sounded good. We decided to use Jim's car, an older Saab, that he said was up to the challenge.

By the time we were ready to leave, we had two cars and eight kids going to Florida. I rode shotgun in Jim's Saab and we followed Dave and his group in their 1965 Ford Mustang. Our little caravan left Flint, heading south down I-75 to the Sunshine State. We passed the time talking over our plans and the many girls we would surely meet. We stopped for lunch and, so far, everything was going great.

What a super idea this trip was!

But trouble found us when we hit Lima, Ohio. Jim's Saab broke down and we barely managed to push it off the expressway and onto the shoulder. We looked under the hood and tinkered, but to no avail.

Dave stopped with his group to see if they could help, but now it was getting late in the day and a decision had to be made.

We told Dave to continue on to Florida and enjoy spring break. Jim and I would try to fix the Saab and join them.

Dave reluctantly agreed. One of the guys from our car squeezed into Dave's Mustang. That left Jim, Louie and me on the side of the road next to Jim's broken-down car.

We had our sleeping bags, backpacks, and a few bucks between us. Jim and Louie with their long hair and ragged beards, and I with a couple of days' stubble, looked like bums. Abandoning the Saab, we walked into a small town just outside of Lima where we ate dinner at a tiny hole-in-the-wall cafe.

Afterwards, we headed into the town. We met some kids near a small park and told them our sad story. We also might have mentioned that we would be sleeping under the town railroad bridge, roasting hot dogs and drinking beer. We had neither—real big shots.

A little while later, as we headed toward the bridge, a police car pulled over and stopped us. A mean-looking policeman wearing a tan uniform, sunglasses, and wide-brim cowboy hat asked us where we were headed.

We repeated our story and he looked unimpressed, asking if we intended to sleep under the railroad bridge.

I was surprised. How did he know?

Those darn kids.

We told him, "No, sir!"

He said that was good, adding in a very menacing, authoritarian voice, "You boys get the hell out of my town and don't you come back! You hear?"

We nodded and must have said, "Yes, sir!" a dozen times as we retreated rapidly down the road toward the city limits.

Well, we were run out of town. We had a couple of bucks, no place to sleep, and it was getting dark. We walked a little farther and through the trees, I saw a drive-in movie theater. The cars were all in place and the first feature had just begun. Behind the drive-in was a farmer's field and that sparked an idea.

We cut through the farmer's field near the back edge of the drive-in. Spreading our sleeping bags in the tall grass, we settled in and watched the movie. At some point, we drifted off to sleep.

In the morning, we awoke to cows mooing and munching grass all around us. We stretched, rolled up our sleeping bags, and headed back to the expressway.

Mike standing by Jim's Saab on I-75 in a traffic jam.

All day, we tried hitching a ride on the expressway ramp. No one was interested in picking up three scraggly looking bums. It was late in the day and we were awfully hungry. Pooling our money, we ate a meager dinner at another hole-in-the-wall. Afterwards, we headed back to the drive-in and settled in to sleep. It started to rain.

The next morning, we bade a soggy farewell to the cows and headed back to the on-ramp. We tried hitching again without success. With everyone speeding past us, how would we ever get a ride? And that's when my creative problem solving went into overdrive.

I told Jim and Louie to line up with me, like a chorus line. On the count of three, we would all stick out our thumbs in unison with a big smile, just like on television.

One, two, three—Smile!

No luck.

Another car was coming. One, two, three—Smile!

The car stopped and we were in shock. It was a station wagon with bundles tied on top. We ran up to the passenger door and a nice lady asked where we were headed. Her husband was driving and he leaned across the seat, looking us over.

We exclaimed in unison, "Flint!"

The driver said, "So are we. Hop in, boys."

We all crammed into the back seat and the car started down the ramp. We were going home!

The driver introduced himself, his wife, and their little daughter who was riding in front with them. We introduced ourselves and thanked him profusely for picking us up.

He said, "That's okay. We're glad to help."

He asked us where we lived and I explained that my apartment was on First Street while Jim and Louie lived a couple of blocks over.

He said he was familiar with the location and he kindly volunteered to drop us off at our homes.

We were so grateful that we pooled our little remaining money and offered it to him for gas.

"No, boys. You put that money in the church basket on Sunday."

We thanked him and promised we would.

It was a long but very pleasant ride home. We never made it to Florida for spring break. Dave and his crew did, and they had many wild tales to tell. We had tales, also—only ours involved cows.

—⁓—

Just before Christmas break, I got into big trouble at the factory. My right hand had been bandaged (I don't remember how I hurt it) but it didn't affect my job performance.

Later that morning, I was feeling tired and a little sorry for myself because my hand hurt. I wanted to take a break but we'd already had our morning break. So lunchtime would be my next chance.

Not wanting to wait, I decided to work down the line to create time so I could take an unauthorized break. I took my tools and walked down the line to the point where the cars were arriving, and quickly did my tasks on each car body.

If this were done properly and no one caught you, then you could create a bubble in the line where all the cars coming to your station would already be finished.

This practice worked well for two cars, giving the person who performed it about three minutes to go to the rest room or grab a smoke. Of course, this procedure was highly illegal. If a worker on the line needed to take an unscheduled break, he flagged down his foreman who sent in a roving substitute to keep the line moving.

Asking to have someone spell you for a nap was not an approved break. I had never tried this maneuver on more than two cars, but that day, I decided to do ten! At the pace the cars were moving, that would give me about fifteen minutes and I could grab my quick nap. Why I didn't stop and think this through, I'll never know. I guess we all do stupid things.

I told Tommy I was working down the line and took off. I kept a sharp eye out for foremen and worked furiously on each car body all the way back to the welding stations. I set my gloves on top of the last car body I had worked on and quickly returned to my station.

Telling Tommy to wake me when he saw my gloves coming down the line, I immediately crawled behind some cardboard boxes by my station and went to sleep.

I awoke to someone yelling very loudly. I was a little confused, not quite knowing where I was. So I poked my head up over the boxes to see what was going on and what I saw terrified me!

Standing by my workstation and surrounding Tommy were about ten men in white shirts with skinny black ties and in the middle of them all was my foreman, Art.

A big guy in a white shirt was doing all the screaming. I found out later it was Mr. Johnson, the floor supervisor; the big boss with his posse of engineers.

Mr. Johnson was screaming at Art and Tommy. His face was red and everyone looked really scared.

I heard him yell, "The blankety-blank is not even here!"

At that moment, I must have moved because he looked over and saw my sleepy head poking out from behind the pile of boxes.

It was almost comical—for a split second. He looked like he didn't know what he was seeing and he did a double take. Then the realization slid over his face like a dark cloud.

He bellowed, "The blankety-blank-blank was sleeping!"

I was ordered to stand front and center while Mr. Johnson took about five minutes to scream at me at the top of his lungs. His face was almost purple and spit flew from his mouth. He called me the most incredibly foul, dirty names; some of which I'd never heard before!

He ended his tirade by yelling, "You're fired! Clean out your locker at the end of the shift and get off the property!"

He told Art to make it happen and he and his group left to unsnarl the damage I had caused.

Art talked gently to me, like a father, telling me he was real sorry to see me go. He explained that by my working on those cars away from my station in such a hurry, I did not properly do all of my assigned tasks. Every one of them had to be pulled off the line and re-worked because the windshields would not fit. All because I wanted so badly to take a nap.

This snafu had created a break in the line and idled the entire plant for those fifteen minutes. Lots of money was lost.

I could hardly comprehend the massive train wreck I had caused. I felt sick over having let down both Art and Tommy. I had screwed up big time and deserved to be fired.

I returned to work and silence hung over our little workstation like a thick black cloud. Tommy seemed really sad and avoided looking at me. We ate lunch without talking and went back to work when the line started up.

Sometime after lunch, a small man in a black and white leather jacket with big UAW letters and a round, union gear logo on the back approached my station. He timed his visit to coincide with our afternoon break and he called me over.

He lit up a Camel and explained that he was my union rep. He understood that I was in big trouble with the management.

I told him about the cars being pulled off the line, confessing that it was all my fault, and that I'd been fired.

He cut me off and said, "Don't ever say it was your fault!! Now tell me what happened."

He smoked as I told him my story. I could tell by his expression that it was really bad; that there was nothing he could do for me. In short order, I had really screwed this up.

At the end of my story, he said, "Tell me exactly what Mr. Johnson said to you."

I was embarrassed to say some of the words Mr. Johnson had used so he prompted me with some questions.

"Did he call you a blankety-blank, and a blankety-blank-blank?"

"Yes."

The rep looked at the floor, thinking; cigarette smoke drifted around his head like a wreath. When he finally looked up at me, he was smiling.

He said, "Kid, stand by your station at quitting time and I'll meet you here."

He left and I went back to work for my last couple of hours. At the end of the shift, the siren blew, and the line stopped. Tommy was getting ready to say his goodbyes when I noticed a large group of men walking toward me. I felt like running but fear glued me to the floor.

There were about five men in white shirts and black skinny ties and about five men in leather UAW union jackets, all heading right for me. In the middle of this group were Mr. Johnson, Art, and the union rep I spoke with earlier.

The group stopped and formed a half circle around me. Mr. Johnson stood directly in front of me, flanked on either side by Art and the union rep. Mr. Johnson looked like he had swallowed a big slug of castor oil; he looked sick.

He was struggling to get something out, and I could see the tension in his face, his blood vessels were bulging blue lines on his red face.

He was staring over my head and finally growled through clenched teeth, "I'm sorry!"

Immediately, the entire group except for Art and the union rep turned and departed.

The union rep chuckled and said, "Kid, your job is safe; you ain't fired. But don't screw up no more!" And with that he turned and left.

It seems that Mr. Johnson had every right to fire me, but he could not call me those foul names, and that was what the union used to save my job.

Art looked at me and it was hard to return his gaze. I knew I had messed up.

He said, "Kid, looks like you have a second chance; don't waste it. See you tomorrow."

I learned a very valuable lesson. I was wrong. I should have been fired, but I was given a second chance and I did learn from it.

Christmas break was the next week and the entire plant shut down. When I came back after the holiday, I went to my locker where Art was waiting for me. He told me that I had been transferred to a new station with a new foreman—all thanks to Mr. Johnson.

I said goodbye to Tommy and Art escorted me to my new workstation. Mr. Johnson could not fire me but he did get his revenge. He had me moved to a station that was right outside the doors of the heat furnace through which the car bodies moved for some type of treatment.

My new job was to climb into the car bodies as they came out and screw four bolts into the transmission cover on the floor. This seemed like easy work until I did it for a while. The climbing in and out of all those car bodies was tough on both joints and clothes.

I wore out a pair of work gloves every shift just screwing in the bolts. This job was no fun! I was also all by myself with no one to talk to. The noise, the heat, and the constant motion made for a really hard workday. Mr. Johnson passed by, unsmiling, every now and then to check up on me.

—∿—

About a week into my new job, the word went through the plant that Art had passed away at home from a massive heart attack. About a week later, we went through a series of layoffs and I was laid off, thus ending my fledgling career as an assembly line worker.

To be honest, I missed the money but not the shop! The last day on the line, I decided to celebrate. While on break, I bought a cigarillo for a nickel from a vending machine and went back to the line to smoke it.

Never having smoked before, for some strange reason, I wanted to try it. I was such a novice. I couldn't light the cigar because I didn't have any matches! I heated a piece of metal to red hot on a grinder and fired up my smoke.

I coughed and spit and thought it was awful. The nicotine was already working its terrible magic in my system. I wished I'd never bought that first cigar!

Immediately after I left the shop, a man at our church hired me to work at his small engineering and surveying firm. I worked there part-time as a draftsman doing mostly cut and fill sections for a new highway.

My job was to figure out the amount of fill material (dirt added) or cut (dirt removed) from cross-section drawings of a road project. I enjoyed the work, learning a lot from the regular draftsmen in the company. My part-time schedule worked well with my college schedule. I was with this firm for a couple of months until their road project was finished and I was laid off.

CHAPTER NINE

I didn't let any grass grow under my feet.
I had bills to pay! So as soon as I was laid off from that small engineering firm, I scoured the newspaper for job listings. I saw an ad in *The Flint Journal* for a draftsman in the Flint Water Department.

I was going to school full-time in the spring of 1970 at Mott Community College, and with my major in Mechanical Design Technology, I had lots of drafting classes. Based on course studies and my brief employment with the engineering firm, I figured I was qualified for the job.

The Flint Water Department was located in the southeast part of the city—the outskirts of town in the early 1970s. This main location included the office building, pumping stations, water tower, and administration, and it covered several acres.

The job that interested me was physically located in a separate building about ten miles south of the main plant. This department was responsible for making and updating the maps, blueprints, and plans required for the laying and repair of all city water lines. They had a small engineering and surveying section, a hydrant and water meter repair section, and service line repair crews. The bulk of the department handled waterline laying and repair.

The whole department was housed in a long, single-story building. On one end were two offices, a drafting section with a break room, and a locker room with showers. A long hallway connected this end of the building to the maintenance garage where all of the trucks and heavy equipment were repaired.

There were several small shops along the hallway for meter and hydrant repair. The maintenance garage opened onto a concrete court-yard with storage sheds directly across from it. Backhoes, trailers, ser-vice trucks, and dump trucks were housed here. The whole complex was on about three acres off of a very quiet city street on the outskirts of town.

I drove to this location, parked my car in the employee parking lot, and walked in the front door to apply in person. A secretary greeted me and I asked to apply for the draftsman job.

I sat in the lobby, filled out the application, and handed it back. The lobby was very small—two chairs facing each other along with the receptionist's desk. There were two office doors behind her on either side. She asked me to take a seat and went into the office on the right.

A few minutes later, she emerged and invited me into the office. Mr. Pierotti, the head engineer, greeted me. Shaking my hand, he motioned to a chair, and promptly launched into the interview.

I was a little uneasy because I hadn't expected to be interviewed on the spot; I thought I was just dropping off my application.

Mr. Pierotti put me at ease and started telling me about the water department, what they did, and how important the work was. He occa-sionally asked me a question, but he did most of the talking.

Smoking was allowed in almost every office and building at that time. Mr. Pierotti's pipe filled his office with an aromatic blue smoke. Through the haze, I noticed the contrast of his thick, black, wavy hair, black-framed glasses and black necktie against his bright white shirt and pocket protector full of pens.

He spoke in short, clipped sentences with a definite accent. He was fond of saying, "Yah, yah, yah."

I didn't know it then, but Mr. Pierotti would turn out to be a great boss and an invaluable mentor for me. I sat across from his desk dur-ing my interview. He must have liked what he saw in my short neat haircut, clean-shaven face, and business attire.

After a short discussion, he hired me as a full-time employee and wanted me to start immediately.

But there was a problem because I was also a college student.

He thought about it and reasoned that I could still be hired and work a full forty-hour week. I could clock out, attend classes and return, making up my forty hours by working late in the evening and on weekends. I thought this was great and thanked him. Thus began my career as a draftsman and future surveyor with the Flint Water Department.

There were only three people in the surveying and drafting section. Lou was head surveyor and draftsman, and boss of the survey road gang. He reported directly to Mr. Pierotti.

Lou was tall, lanky, and in his late fifties. From his drafting table immediately outside the blueprint vault at the back of the office, Lou could see the entire section and keep an eye on us.

He smoked constantly and always had a Lucky Strike fired up in the ashtray on the corner of his drafting table. He spoke very soft, perfect English, and his face was crinkled and worn, like polished leather.

He peered at us through thick glasses, like he was trying to figure us (or something) out while absently taking a pull on his cigarette. Lou turned out to be a good teacher for me, but a lousy role model for smoking and drinking.

Ronnie, the other draftsman in the department, was in his early thirties. He was the playboy of the office and drove nice, newer cars. I got the impression that he only wanted the job for the money and really didn't care much about the work. He and Lou seemed to be at odds most of the time and rarely spoke.

Ronnie's drafting table was directly behind mine. To talk to him, all I had to do was swivel around and lean on his table. My drafting table was right outside Mr. Pierotti's office.

Lou took me around the whole department and introduced me to everyone. There were about forty employees—most of them in the repair, maintenance, service, and pipe sections.

Mr.Walters, who was probably in his early sixties, ran the entire department. He had a full head of white hair and always wore a light beige sport coat. His office was bigger than Mr. Pierotti's and nearer to Mary's reception desk.

Mr. Walters never spoke to me and he acted like he had no time for me. He stayed in his office, spoke with Mr. Pierotti, Mary, and a few others, but mostly left us alone. That was just fine with me.

Lou showed me to my desk, helped me with drafting supplies and gave me the lowdown on how he ran the office. He started me out with easy work—updating the locations of water shutoff valves on the master city blueprints.

City water workers were sent out to a residence or company to resolve a water supply issue. It was most often a broken service line between the main line and the residence. This usually required them to shut off the water to the house at the master shut off valve, located somewhere between the curb and the sidewalk.

If the valve location was not obvious, they checked their maps and blueprints for the 'as built' location. If the valve still couldn't be found, they had to locate it with a hand-held magnetometer.

Once found, they took distance measurements from known locations to the valve and recorded the new location along with a sketch in their notes. At the end of their shift, they turned in these notes to Lou. He checked them and then turned them over to me to update the master vellum blueprint.

I had a ton of these notes to work on. I later learned that updating the master vellums was a low priority. That's why I got them instead of Ronnie. The whole process was time-consuming, tedious, and not too exciting, but it still required precision and attention to detail.

To update a shutoff valve, I took the house address and went into the blueprint vault to look up the appropriate blueprint sheet.

The city was divided into sections. A section was drawn on a large piece of vellum paper, which was like waxed paper cloth. Paper blueprints were run off from these vellum sections on a big blueprint machine located outside the vault.

Once I found the correct section, I took the master vellum from the drawer and left a paper marker so I could replace it correctly. I took the vellum to my table and located the address and street to update. I checked the notes and then carefully erased the old ink information with an electric handheld erasing machine. It was vital not to burn a hole through the vellum.

I then swept the vellum clean with my horsehair drafting brush and got my Rapidograph ink pen. I carefully inked in the measurements from the known location to the updated location of the water valve. I used my circle template to draw a small circle where the valve was actually located, then blew on the ink to dry it.

If I were lucky, I had a few more to do on this sheet while it was out. If not, then back to the vault, replace it, and pull the next one. After a few times doing this, I could see why Lou and Ronnie gave me this work to do.

Lou also had me updating sections of repaired water pipe using the notes from the construction crews. Most of my early work was this type of updating.

When Lou was satisfied with my work ethic and product, he moved me on to other more challenging drafting tasks. I stayed busy, leaving the office to attend classes and then returning to finish my shift.

On my breaks, I often walked the building and ended up in the garage, talking to the mechanics as they worked on the trucks. The department was using 1966 Chevrolet C-60 single axle dump trucks. They were big, orange, and beautiful. I loved watching the guys work on them.

—◊—

Our engineering section was also responsible for all of the surveying and construction plans for new city water lines. This was the work that Lou did and he used Ronnie and me as his survey road gang.

One afternoon, Lou said we were all going out in the field the next day to survey for a new water line off of Clio Road, so we should be sure to wear old clothes and work boots.

I was excited! That night I laid out my clothes and boots and made sure my alarm clock was set. I was going on my first surveying job!

We met at the office and gathered the equipment. Lou carried the theodolite, Ronnie carried the level, and I carried the tripods and survey rod. In the shed, we loaded the equipment into a big tan Chevrolet Suburban carryall.

Lou drove, Ronnie sat in front, and I had the back seat. The drive to the section of road took about twenty minutes. Once we arrived, Lou set up the theodolite and took out his little pocket notebook. Ronnie did the pole work while I cleared brush with a machete and brush hook.

I asked Ronnie to explain the pole work he was doing and he did, but he was more interested in when we would finish. I learned that Ronnie had a different work ethic from mine, and Lou warned me to keep my distance.

Lou looked through the theodolite and then wrote in his little notebook. He signaled Ronnie to move slightly right or left and then waved his arms. That was the cue for Ronnie to mark the spot. We didn't have radios, so we relied on hand signals. Being low man, I lugged the equipment, cut brush, and played "go-for" (go for this, go for that).

I helped Ronnie hold the tape measure, learned how to properly hold the level rod so Lou could read the numbers on it through the level, and of course, learned how to safely cut brush. I also cleaned all of the equipment when we returned to the office.

We did surveying in the spring and summer. I enjoyed the field-work and learning all about it. I asked Lou a lot of questions every chance I got. He saw that I was really interested and began teaching me how to survey. He was a good, patient teacher. He also had me lug the heavy equipment between set-up points.

I learned how to set up the equipment at every new point. Lou taught me how to set up a tripod and place the dumpy level on top, then level the entire piece over a little point on the ground.

Ronnie held the rod that had numbers on it over the next point on the ground and I read the numbers while Lou recorded them.

At first, Lou always checked my readings and corrected me if they were off. Eventually, I did the set ups, readings, and moves to the next location on my own. I kept my own set of readings in my little note-book and did the math when we got back to the office.

These measurements were then turned into drawings. Lou placed the new water line on the drawing as well as all of the other under-ground services like gas, electric, and sewer.

I researched the city records for those lines and other existing water lines. All of these had to be located and drawn exactly as they lay on the new construction drawing. I enjoyed this kind of detailed detective work and marveled at how busy, yet organized, the final drawing was.

Back in the office, Lou checked his notes and mine, and then it would be time to create the construction drawing. We did many of these, such as the one for Hamilton Avenue.

The existing water line on Hamilton was an old 6-inch diameter line that was to be replaced with a new 24-inch main. We pulled the existing blueprints from the map vault.

For these older streets, it was typical that the blueprints were either inadequate or missing. Once we had all the existing data we could find, we then went out in the field and conducted the survey.

Since all of the existing pipes and utilities were already underground and not visible, we did a topographical survey of the entire section of street where the new water line was to be laid.

A topographical survey locates, measures, and marks all manhole covers, sewer basins, fire hydrants, telephone poles, trees and any other type of permanent object in or adjacent to the right-of-way. Everything was recorded in our little survey books with exact measurements and elevations.

We used the one hundred foot steel tape and handheld plumb bobs to measure distances and used the theodolite to record the angles. We used the dumpy level and elevation rod to establish the elevations and record permanent benchmarks for future reference.

We took all of this actual field data (such as locations of sewer manholes, etc.) and cross-checked them with other utility drawings for accuracy.

This work was fast paced and fun. Lou let me set up the instruments for each new shot and I got really good at quickly and accurately setting up the level or theodolite.

Ronnie held the close end of the measuring tape and I hustled the other end to the object we were locating. Once over the object, we pulled the steel tape tight and used a plumb bob to get an exact location. Once I had the measurement, we called out the readings for Lou to mark down. He was always hunkered down over his little book next to the level, with a cigarette in his mouth. On busy streets, we had to watch for cars while running the tape or setting the elevation rod.

I liked being outside on the job. The days went by quickly and we got to eat out for lunch. We all liked Coney Island hotdogs, so we usually stopped at one of the many Greek restaurants in the area. Coney Islands ("Flint style") consisted of a Koegel hot dog in its casing, a steamed bun with loose, crumbly Coney Island sauce, and a line of yellow mustard; all topped off with a mound of white onions. A couple of hotdogs with fries and a Coke from the Starlight Grill and we were ready to get back to work.

When we finished a survey job, Lou let me make the drawings. I started out with simple drawings like the one below for the new water line on Hamilton Avenue.

I took all of the measurements and notes from our books and created the drawing. I placed the new water line in the drawing and generated the bill of materials. The top half of the drawing shows the overhead street view. The bottom half of the drawing shows the profile view. This is how the buried line would look underground if viewed from the side. It gives the depth of burial and heights of the manholes.

Manholes were standard designs and we did not have to show any details. Most valves were also standard and the same rule applied. This job, however, had a special bypass valve that required a separate drawing showing the details of the valve and manhole. The drawing on the following page is an example of some of the more detailed work that I did for the water department.

—◊◊◊—

My college courses and work schedule kept me very busy. In order to get in my forty hours a week, I pulled a lot of weekend hours doing drawings and valve location updates.

On the weekends, there was a man on duty who answered emergency calls to check out water line breaks and shut off water to homes as required. I got to know these guys when they stopped by to talk.

They answered their calls in a big orange Chevrolet box truck that had all of the necessary items they might need for a job. This was a

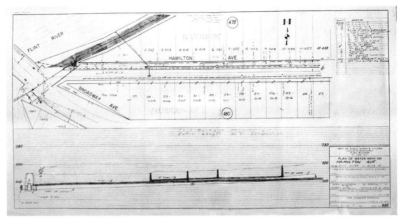

Blueprint, page one of three, for a new 24-inch water main that I drew from my field survey notes. This line was to be installed along Hamilton Avenue.

neat truck because there were only two front seats and the doors slid open so you could ride around town with the doors open on hot days.

Ralph was one of the more colorful meter repairmen. One beautiful, sunny Saturday, he must have felt sorry for my having to work inside, so he asked if I wanted to ride along on some jobs.

I jumped at the chance and followed him down the hallway to the garage where his truck was parked. We climbed aboard, waved to the weekend maintenance men working on a dump truck, and headed out the gate. I was pumped up! I felt important riding around in this orange city truck with its an emergency light on top just waiting to flash a warning to everyone: Men at Work!

We came to a large intersection on Dort Highway and stopped for the red light. We were in the right lane. I saw an old green station wagon with luggage tied to the roof waiting in the left turn lane and facing us across the busy street.

The rear tire was on fire! The brakes had probably locked up and started the blaze. The family was quickly getting out and moving away from the car. The man was looking at the tire in a panic. He didn't have anything at hand to put it out.

I looked by my seat and saw a big red fire extinguisher. I grabbed it and was ready to exit the truck and take action!

Ralph stopped me and said, "Never mind, kid, they'll get it."

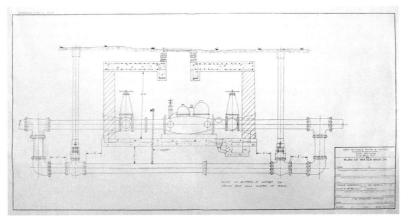

Blueprint of my detailed drawing of the Hamilton Avenue 24-inch water valve with bypass and manhole.

Having said that, he turned right on red and headed away from the car. We traveled about three blocks and made our first stop of the day, the donut shop! I had a peanut crumb donut and coffee. Ralph had his usual and started a conversation with the waitress.

We made several calls that morning and I learned how to shut off water valves. At every stop, I took measurements and notes so I could update the appropriate maps back at the office.

Ralph was a good teacher and I learned a lot. A couple of hours later, we came to that same intersection on Dort Highway and stopped for the red light. Sitting across the street in the same spot was that green station wagon, only it was no longer green. It was a burnt, black, shell of a car. They obviously did not get the fire out and that family lost everything. I looked at Ralph. He shrugged, gave me a sheepish smile, and we headed off to our next call.

—⚒—

I liked to hang out in the maintenance bay on weekends and evenings. Everything we used had a clutch and stick shift. These rough, tough men were always working on vehicles, and they were very capable mechanics.

In the winter of 1970, I was at work on a Saturday after a big snowstorm when one of the mechanics in the maintenance bay said, "Hey, kid, why don't you take that dump truck and plow the snow?"

One of the city dump trucks was fitted with a large front-mounted hydraulic snowplow used to clear the parking areas and storage sites. I didn't have to be asked twice! He quickly gave me a short "how to" talk and sent me on my way.

I opened the door, climbed up into the cab, and looked around. I depressed the clutch with my left foot and started the engine. The big V-8 roared to life with a belch of smoke. As the truck warmed up, I did a few test moves, lifting and lowering the blade and shifting the gears. When I was ready, I went to work. The snow was deep, but it was no match for that big orange dump truck.

The more I practiced plowing, the more my confidence grew. Pushing the snow into large piles, I cleared the empty parking areas, lanes, and road to the street. While maneuvering on the main street to turn around, I made sure the emergency lights and orange, rotating, bubble light on top were flashing.

Backing up one last time, I looked out of the driver's side window as something passed by very, very close. It was the water department mailbox. By some miracle, I just barely missed taking it out. I shifted into first gear and headed back to the shed, feeling very happy and proud of the good work done over the last several hours.

I parked the truck and entered the main building through the maintenance bay to find a surprise awaiting me. One of the meter readers was standing there in his coat, scarf, and earmuff hat holding a silver thermos bottle of coffee. He was loudly complaining to anyone who would listen about how his overtime job was stolen from him. He was supposed to plow the snow!

He saw me come into the bay and stomped over to where I was standing. He told me angrily that I had robbed him of his overtime! Plowing the snow was his job!

I noticed the two mechanics quietly laughing and getting a big kick out of this guy's frustration. I realized they had set me up.

Apologizing to him, I promised it wouldn't happen again and he stormed out.

This incident stayed in the shop and went no further. I learned quickly that no one ever ratted out another employee to the boss; you just worked out your differences.

—⟋⟋⟍—

One day in the spring of 1971, we received word that we were getting new dump trucks. Chevrolet lost the bid to GMC so all our trucks were now GMC's. I remember the day when those new trucks arrived. Everyone was on break in the lunchroom and we all headed for the maintenance bay.

There they were, just delivered, sitting in a row outside the big maintenance door in the bright sunlight. The first thing I noticed was that the nose of these trucks was short, almost squat. This made the cab ride taller on the body.

Our old Chevrolets had long hoods making them look leaner. The new dump trucks looked like mean, orange bulldogs guarding the yard and ready to go to work.

One of the newest employees, Jimmy, ran over to one of the new trucks and said, "This one is mine."

He climbed up into the cab and immediately started looking over the gauges while running his hands over the steering wheel and gearshift lever. I envied him because it would be his truck, working on the construction crew that laid the water lines.

Jimmy was a couple of years older than I was, a high school graduate, and an Army veteran. He'd been drafted and spent a year in Viet Nam. Everyone liked Jimmy and they respected him for serving his country and pulling his combat tour.

I remember the first week he was on the job. A couple of the guys were talking in the break room before evening checkout time.

I overheard one say, "Did you see Jimmy's scars in the shower?"

The other guy said, "Yes."

They talked quietly and respectfully about how he was wounded by a land mine and had horrible scars all over his legs and torso. It was the first time, but not the last, that I would hear of the effects that war left on guys my age.

—⟋⟋⟍—

One day a radio call came in over the main system located just outside our office. A worker was frantically shouting that a trench had collapsed at the water main construction site and Jimmy was buried alive!

Mr. Walters and Mr. Pierotti ran from their offices and spoke to the man on the radio in short, hurried clips. They told Mary to call for emergency services as they ran to their city car, jumped in, and raced to the site.

We left our drafting tables and huddled near the radio, listening to the urgent messages back and forth between the city water workers and the emergency responders. We waited and prayed, staring at the big gray radio by Mary's desk.

Everything was quiet for what seemed an eternity. Finally we heard over the radio that they got him out, and he was alive! I relaxed my shoulders. My body was stiff and I realized I had been anxiously holding my breath.

Thirty minutes later, they had him back in the break room. The workers were covered in dirt and mud. A dazed Jimmy sat at the table looking like he had been pulled from the grave. Dirt streaked all over his face and his hair was matted in globs of muck.

The mud-caked workers huddled around him, patting him on the back, and talking and laughing with him. Mr. Walters joined the celebration and looked relieved.

—⟨⟨⟨—

Safety was very important at the water department. Lou taught me the importance of safety on the survey sites. Namely, always look out for traffic and never trust that the driver sees you.

On the construction sites, he taught me to physically touch the back of the big-tracked power shovel that was digging. Regardless of the direction from which we approached, the equipment operator could not hear us, and sometimes he could not see us. By touching the side or back of the cab, you could feel the shovel move, and that movement would give you the warning you needed to get out of the way.

—⟨⟨⟨—

I felt like I had a home at the water department. I had moved out of my parents' house at eighteen and never went back.

My dad retired from the fire station in 1971, leaving me as the only one in the family with an active City job. I liked living in the city, but I was starting to look for better accommodations.

Lou invited me over to his house for dinner on several occasions. We sat on his small front porch, smoking cigarettes and drinking his favorite beer, Pabst Blue Ribbon. Lou had a small Chihuahua that he always held on his lap like a baby. That dog was mean. He constantly barked and bared his teeth at me.

Lou said with a laugh, "He likes you, but just don't try to pet him."

It was in these off-work settings that he told me whom I could trust and whom I should stay away from at work. I didn't know it then, but Lou was mentoring me. He was a good boss and he cared about me. He was giving me insights garnered from his life's work experience to help me and I soaked up his words of wisdom.

We had a time clock in the lunchroom where we all punched in and out. The employees lined up about five minutes before the end of the shift, holding their card from the rack in front of the machine.

There was always a lot of banter, joking, and horsing around in the line. The time clock bell rang at 4:30 p.m. sharp, signaling punch out time. Punching out even one minute early meant being docked a quarter of an hour.

One night, exactly one minute before the clock rang, the man at the front of the line reached up inside the time clock and manually rang the bell. He then pretended to punch out and started to walk away.

The next three guys in line clocked out before one of them realized they were really one minute early! The joker started laughing and words flew. Before you knew it, a big brawl erupted and punches were thrown. Suddenly, it wasn't funny anymore.

Just then the time clock actually rang 4:30 and the remainder of the guys punched out and headed out the door, grumbling. The three guys lost a quarter of an hour and I didn't stick around to see how it all ended.

I liked my job and I was thinking of making it my career. I still thought that I wanted to join the Army, but how could I do that and stay with the City?

One day, I turned around from my drafting table and started talking with Ronnie about how to move up in the water department. Lou was out of the office on an errand so the timing was good.

"So when Lou retires—do you get Lou's job and I get yours?"

Ronnie laughed and said, "No, that's not how it works. When Lou retires in a few years, they'll run an ad in *The Flint Journal* and they'll get over two hundred applications for his job. The chances of my getting it are slim to none."

This did not sit well with me because there appeared no way for me to move up the ladder. I started thinking of my other option, the Army. I was close to graduation from college in a few months and if I were going to join the Army, that would be the time to do it.

Now it never occurred to me to talk to my bosses about my career path. I had just gotten the scoop. Or had I?

Think about it. I had just asked for career advice from a guy who was not very motivated and not in charge. Big mistake? Maybe. Maybe not. I needed the unintentional shove that he gave me to finalize my career plans.

I had been working full time now for over a year while carrying a heavy class schedule at the community college. My active social life kept the candle burning at both ends. I would graduate in late June of 1971 with my associate's degree in Mechanical Design Technology.

Lou had given me on-the-job training and I was a fairly accomplished surveyor. He was even letting me take the survey truck out solo to do follow-up work.

I was happy with my job, but the apparent lack of upward mobility with the City kept nagging at me.

I graduated from college that summer and decided to seriously consider enlisting in the Army. So one sunny afternoon, I went into the recruiter's office in Flint. This one meeting changed my life. I signed up to be a combat engineer in the United States Army.

The guys at the City threw a farewell party for me on my last day at work. Everyone was there and we had a cake and drinks in the cafeteria. Lou presented me with a gift from the group. I opened it to find a very nice transistor radio. He said I could listen to it as I sat on my footlocker cleaning my rifle. Everyone laughed and we had a good time.

I felt sad to be leaving such a wonderful bunch of guys, but was also excited and curious about the future.

I tied up any loose ends in Flint, said goodbye to some girls, and visited my parents. A few of my belongings were left at their home in Flushing, including my .22 rifle.

Having sold my car, I went to catch the bus to Fort Knox, Kentucky, and Basic training. I was going on a fully paid two-year vacation, compliments of Uncle Sam!

Little did I know that I would spend the next thirty-three years of my life in the Army, starting out as a private E-1 and retiring with the rank of colonel O-6. But that's another story.

ACKNOWLEDGMENTS

To Lynne, thank you for your love and support.

To Jim, sixty years and counting, and still best friends.

To my brothers, Ken, Bob, John, and Don, we survived and had fun along the way.

To my sister, Mary, for your cameo appearance in this "boys' world" book, love you.

To Rick Michael and Tom Montpas, thank you for having my back.

To my dad, for instilling an honest work ethic in me.

To my mom, for letting us play outside. In retrospect, that may have been an act of self-defense.

To my Grandpa Klein, for all the wonderful memories of exploring and pretending at your farm.

To Aunt Francis, for being a second mom to me when I was just a little tyke.

To Aunt Joanne, who provided me with our family history so I could write this book.

To Elaine, for your eagle-eye editing and for helping me tell my story.

To Jan, for bringing your publishing expertise to this project.

To Mott Community College, for making my military career possible.

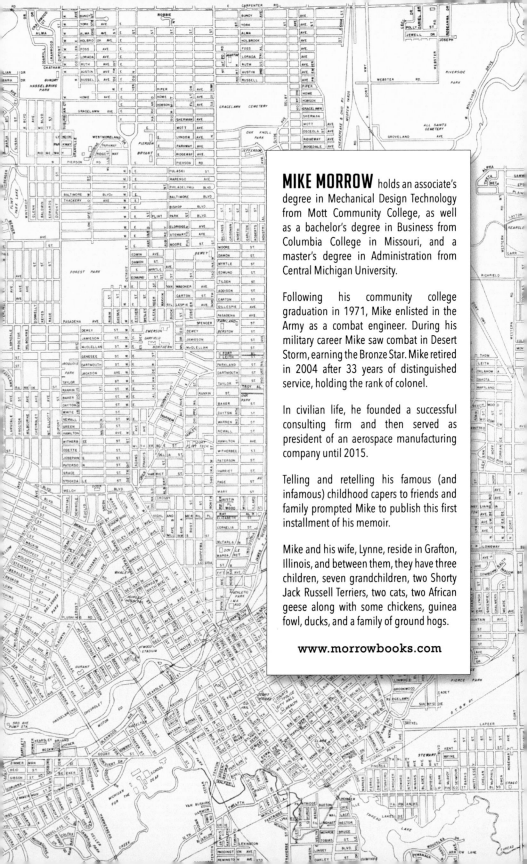

MIKE MORROW holds an associate's degree in Mechanical Design Technology from Mott Community College, as well as a bachelor's degree in Business from Columbia College in Missouri, and a master's degree in Administration from Central Michigan University.

Following his community college graduation in 1971, Mike enlisted in the Army as a combat engineer. During his military career Mike saw combat in Desert Storm, earning the Bronze Star. Mike retired in 2004 after 33 years of distinguished service, holding the rank of colonel.

In civilian life, he founded a successful consulting firm and then served as president of an aerospace manufacturing company until 2015.

Telling and retelling his famous (and infamous) childhood capers to friends and family prompted Mike to publish this first installment of his memoir.

Mike and his wife, Lynne, reside in Grafton, Illinois, and between them, they have three children, seven grandchildren, two Shorty Jack Russell Terriers, two cats, two African geese along with some chickens, guinea fowl, ducks, and a family of ground hogs.

www.morrowbooks.com

Northern portion of 1950s Flint, Michigan
map courtesy of the personal collection of the Morrow family